Goss China
Arms, Decorations
and their values

The Peace Plate. A 205mm crinkle edge plate with a multi-coloured design issued to commemorate Peace in 1919.

Goss China
Arms, Decorations
and their values

Nicholas Pine

Milestone Publications

By the same author
'The Price Guide to Goss China'
'The Price Guide to Crested China'

Published and distributed by
Milestone Publications,
Goss & Crested China Ltd.,
62 Murray Road, Horndean,
Hants, PO8 9JL
Telephone Horndean (0705) 597440

Design Brian Iles
Photography Michael Edwards

ISBN No. 0 903852 24 1

First printed 1979
Revised 1982

Printing by Princo B.V., Culemborg, The Netherlands.

Contents

Acknowledgements

It will be appreciated that to attempt to compile a complete list of all the Arms and Decorations found on Goss China is an enormous task. I have endeavoured to ensure that all available information is included in this volume, and owe an enormous debt of gratitude to Mr. Michael J.W. Willis-Fear, M.A. (Dunelm) who has graciously made available the relevant portions of the thesis which earned him his Master of Arts Degree in 1970. Michael Willis-Fear was one of the earlier Goss collectors. Starting while still at school, he assembled a very fine collection before Goss China enjoyed its current popularity. In 1965 he wrote a twenty-four page treatise for the University of Newcastle-upon-Tyne Philosophical Society entitled, "The History of the Pottery Firm of W.H. Goss of Stoke-on-Trent", together with a review of some of the wares produced, (a booklet long out of print).

For his Master of Arts Degree he set about seeking out and assembling all the available information he could which, together with much original research and some assistance from existing collectors, resulted in a well-illustrated thesis of over six hundred pages!

It is to this thesis that I have been given access, and allowed to draw from the material contained in the sections dealing with Arms and Other Decorations. His basic material was taken from 55 copper plates, the three surviving Goss pattern books, and about 50 wooden framed glass pictures of transfers, all of which were at that time in the possession of Allied English Potteries Ltd., and to this he added information which he had accumulated over the years.

This newly revised volume also incorporates vast amounts of additional data which has been collected by Mr. Dan Scott, who has systematically recorded details of every item he has seen over the last ten or more years, and to whom the author is particularly indebted. In addition, I appreciate being able to draw on the list of pictorial items compiled by the Goss Collectors' Club from information supplied by its several hundred members.

Further information has been obtained from the Club's various Auction lists and correspondence columns, and also from the sales lists published by Goss & Crested China Ltd. and its predecessors. I would also like to thank those individual collectors who have contributed to the book.

I also wish to thank Peter Tranter who has also made available his extensive lists and much other information which has proved to be invaluable.

The transfer printed pictorial views and many other sections have been greatly improved by Paul Dobson. His meticulous work undertaken on behalf of the Goss Collectors' Club has proved invaluable and the author is especially grateful for his assistance.

In addition, Enid and Ray Smith, Christine Love and John Varley have provided much useful information.

I am especially grateful to John Galpin for his assistance in the compilation and expert advice throughout the writing of the book, without which many errors would still remain uncorrected.

This section would not be complete without reference to the work of John D. Magee who did so much to re-popularise Goss wares during the early 1970's, after they had spent some forty years in decline. He carried out much research and unearthed a vast amount of new information which has been incorporated both into this work and into its sister production, 'The Price Guide to Goss China'.

John Magee's enthusiasm for Goss fired many people and no one who ever visited his London premises is ever likely to forget the experience.

Finally, I wish to thank Norman Pratten who has undertaken the 1982 revisions of this book for Milestone Publications: a task which has been carried out with great care and dedication.

Introduction

With the popularity of Goss China now firmly re-established since the demise of the factory around 1930, collectors have specialized as much in arms and decorations as they have the particular models and shapes. It is with this in mind that this work has been produced.

Some 7,000 different arms and decorations will be found itemised in what is, in essence, a massive and exhaustively researched list of every design known.

There will undoubtedly be some omissions from this list as the range of the Goss factory never ceases to amaze. However, for the purposes of buying and selling one must not assume that any arms not found within these covers are valuable, or for that matter any rarer.

Obviously, however, any unrecorded military, commemorative or transfer decorations will have a value slightly in excess of the upper end of the price range shown in a particular section.

The values given throughout the book are an indication of the premium that a particular decoration would attract over the price of a piece with arms of no particular note.

Readers are strongly advised to obtain the sister publication to this work, 'The Price Guide to Goss China' by Nicholas Pine (available from Milestone Publications) as that book is used as a base reference for the value of a particular piece.

To obtain the value of a piece bearing a specific decoration, it should first be located in the Price Guide. To the value so obtained the plusage shown in this work should be added. It will be noted that in many sections only a guide to values is given. It should be stressed that this book is not a Price Guide but values are provided for general guidance. The prices of particular decorations vary so much from person to person that the author would not presume to put a particular price on all the 7,000 or so entries in this book. In addition, if this were done, the book would rapidly become out of date and thus the values would be misleading, as the mere appearance of such a priced list would move the market in many individual pieces — up or down! However, whether prices move either way in the future, the comparative prices between items should remain accurate.

No factory marks are shown in this work as a complete list will be found in 'The Price Guide to Goss China' by Nicholas Pine.

Many early coats-of-arms appear un-named. These will usually be found to be Oxford or Cambridge Colleges as, of course, students of the respective colleges did not need to be told what they were! A little research at the local library will quickly reward the enquirer with such information. Alternatively, many of these college coats-of-arms will be found named on the base of the piece concerned, as the factory originally named many coats-of-arms thus. When Adolphus, the eldest son of William Henry Goss, began to popularize these pieces however, the title was removed from the base and added underneath the 'shield' or other device on the front of the model as shown in many illustrations on other pages.

This book does not attempt to explain heraldry nor does it describe any arms in heraldic terms, or give the history of particular coats-of-arms. This and much similar information will be found in the vast range of books on Heraldry that exist. No attempt at a bibliography is made as there are so many works on the subject that those truly interested will have no difficulty in obtaining copies. However, those interested in heraldry may like to obtain a copy of 'Burke's Peerage' or similar, as many of the arms that the Goss factory used will be found within its pages.

It is worthy of mention here that the occasional spelling mistake crept into the descriptions of arms. For example, Whaley Monastery should be spelt Whalley. In addition, odd letters were occasionally left out of words: for example, Westminste appears without the 'r'. It is possible that such items were sold as seconds. Many pieces were exported and sold abroad by foreign or commonwealth agencies. Such pieces may be found with the words, 'Importe d'Angleterre' on the base (but not always). Items so marked would not be worth any more, so resist the temptations of ignorant dealers who make claims as to the rarity of such pieces and add extortionate premiums to their prices!

Damage is as important to Goss China as it is to stamps, coins or medals. In other words, the slightest chip or crack, a faded crest or rubbed gilding, will affect the value of a piece, unless it is very rare or otherwise desirable, by a great deal. All the values shown in this book are for perfect decorations only. However, in addition to fading in coats-of-arms (to which the blues are particularly prone) oxidization can also occur.

Over a period of years of being exposed to the atmosphere, a crest may go very dull and appear to be faded. Red is the worst colour for appearing to be disfigured in this way but yellow, green and many other colours can also be affected.

Decorations affected thus have a film of a somewhat hard and greasy substance covering them. This can, however, easily be removed by gentle rubbing with household dish-washing liquid or a mild detergent heavily diluted in water, then rinsed thoroughly. The decorations can thus be restored to their former glory quite harmlessly and without showing any signs of deterioration.

Every effort has been made to break down the vast amount of available information into a number of logical sections to assist collectors in their researches, being all the time conscious that there must be many decorations that are still to be recorded. Details of any arms or decorations not in this book will be greatly appreciated by the publishers who will, hopefully, issue a supplementary list in due course.

Details of any new 'finds' will be recorded in 'Goss & Crested China', the monthly catalogue published by Goss & Crested China Ltd, and available from Milestone Publications by annual subscription.

This revised edition contains some 200 additional entries relating to decorations which have come to light since the first edition of this book was published in 1979. Over 75 of these additions are transfer printed views, new examples of which come to light almost weekly. Many of the prints now have colours noted as the decorations have subsequently been seen.

If you cannot find an entry for a decoration in this book read on . . . .

Collectors often fail to find particular arms or decorations and excitedly report them to Milestone as new finds. This must be partly my fault in not making the layout clear enough, but in defence I would say that many entries could appear under more than one heading and I have chosen the most correct in my opinion.

A few suggestions here may help the reader to look in every possible chapter.

Type of Arms:

	Chapters to look under
Personal	B C E F G M N.7
Place Names	A D E F H N.7
Commemoratives	F G H M N

After looking carefully through all of the book, should any decoration not be found listed, please let Milestone Publications have details.

The Peace Plate

An extract from the Pottery Gazette and Glass Trade Review October 1, 1919

By kind permission of Stoke-on-Trent Central Library

Mr. W.H. Goss, Stoke-on-Trent, of original heraldic ivory porcelain fame, continues to hold his lead in the matter of miniatures, souvenir wares and crested novelties, which lines his factory has so long produced with faultless precision in the making and undoubted good taste from a decorative point of view. A visit paid to his factory recently assured one that there is no danger of the Goss reputation losing any of its start, for the very best that is to be had in heraldic wares is still sought and obtained from this maker.

In spite of a succession of difficulties of no uncertain order, Mr. Goss has continued to initiate new lines during and since the war, and thus maintained the interest of his very numerous clients. Whilst speaking of new lines, we would like to call special attention to the accompanying illustration of what we regard as a very fine line in peace commemorative ware.

In the illustration will be seen a wonderfully executed piece —an ivory china plaque—which is supplied in three sizes, 8-inch, 9-inch and 10-inch. It is almost unnecessary to say much in the way of comment upon this photograph, except to emphasise the point that the colours employed are of rare richness and purity, applied with freedom and vigour, and producing an effect equal to all the high traditions of the Goss factory. Turquoise blue is largely dominant in the general decorative effect, and this is a colour which, when well carried out, is always something for the eye to rest upon.

One is hardly likely to tire of a Peace souvenir of this description, for the more one seems to examine it critically the more it seems to reveal in the matter of detail. In the outer wreath of the design one notices, for instance, a long list of names of famous Generals who served during the war on the side of the Allies. It would have been manifestly impossible to have included all the long list of those whose generalship was worthy of being recorded in this way, but clearly a good deal of careful thought has been bestowed by the designer upon the selection. Then again, the arrangement of the Allied flags and the colouring seem to call for a word or two. The Union Jack takes a central position, first of all, obviously because the souvenir is a British production, and possibly also because of the fact that the part played by the British Empire in the Great War has been second to none in the direction of helping to win the war. America

and France follow in sequence, then Belgium and Italy, Serbia and Montenegro, Japan and Greece, Portugal and Roumania. In the lettering at the foot of the design credit is given to the whole of the Allies, one column being devoted to Great Britain and her Dependencies and another column to the Allies of other nationalities. The whole conception is really extremely fine.

It ought to be pointed out, perhaps, that the names of the conspicuous Generals enclosed in the outer wreath are not intended to be placed in any definite order; in fact, they have been indiscriminately inserted intentionally, with the exception, probably, of Haig and Foch, and no one would deny them the greater share of publicity with which they are credited in the larger lettering and the central grouping at the foot of the long list.

Attention is also directed to the fact that both the Army and the Navy figure in the picture with quite a touch of realism. These commemorative plaques are offered by Mr. Goss at a price that is exceptionally moderate when one reflects the enormous amount of detail work which they involve, and, according to the usual principle of the house of Goss, the sale of this novelty will be withdrawn definitely and ruthlessly immediately the usual regulation period has expired, so that it is up to the dealer to make arrangements without delay to satisfy his requirements.

We congratulate Mr. Goss on having produced recently a number of other interesting smalls, some of which appealed to us very forcibly on the occasion of our recent visit to the factory. Mr. Goss is undoubtedly actuated by a goodly measure of individualism in his potting, and prefers to give a lead than to following one. It would not be a disadvantage if other makers of novelty wares would try to do the same.

See Frontispiece

A Short History of
W. H. Goss and his Works

From the turn of the century until virtually the commence-ment of World War Two, souvenir shops almost invariably displayed a wide range of 'crested' china — little white pots and vases bearing the coats-of-arms of the local town, prominent features, or people of note connected with the area.

It is now generally accepted that the finest and most handsomely-decorated of these souvenirs were produced by the firm of W.H. Goss. It would not then, be in-appropriate to include a few details of the man and his work.

William Henry Goss was born in London in 1833, and studied Art at the Government School of Design, then at Somerset House. His daughter, Eva Adeline, tells us that his early working days were spent at W.T. Copeland's porcelain manufacturing firm at Stoke-on-Trent, where, by 1857, he achieved the position of chief designer and modeller.

In 1858, the 25-year old Goss left Copeland's and set up in business on his own account. Understandably, the earlier products of the Goss factory showed the influence of Copeland's work, and a steel-plate engraving in Llewellyn Jewitt's "Ceramic Art in Great Britain" (published in 1878) gives an excellent impression of some of this early work. Goss produced a wide range of ornamental parian ware — vases, urns, figures, groups, etc., and such was the success of his work that his display at the 1862 International Exhibition in London, earned him a Bronze Medallion.

In 1867, Goss entered into partnership, which was to last less than a year, with John Peake, a roofing-tile manufacturer. Terra-cotta was Peake's forte, and the factory used this reddish-brown base for a wide range of tobacco-jars, water-bottles, vases, and jardinieres. As late as 1876, Goss used terra-cotta for his famous "Keystones of the Kingdom" — almost life-sized heads of Lords Beaconsfield and Derby on keystone shaped mounts.

In 1872, Goss perfected and patented several improvements to the manufacturing of jewelled porcelain, which, together with the recently-introduced series of parian busts seems to have prompted the firm's move to larger premises. But tastes were changing, and the 1880's saw a decline in the product-ion of the larger and more costly items, and the gradual introduction of the heraldic porcelain for which Goss is best remembered today. Heraldic porcelain had already been produced, but limited only to the arms of University

Colleges, a few of the better-known public schools, and of certain famous people.

It was at the suggestion of Adolphus, Goss' eldest son, who had joined the firm in 1883, that a whole range of models of historical interest was introduced, each carrying the appropriate coats-of-arms of a town or seaside resort. While the public of those days knew and cared little for heraldry, the attraction to the "day-tripper" of a small porcelain souvenir (costing about a shilling) was well-nigh irresistable! And so with the ever-increasing popularity of "days out" and "trips to the seaside" a whole new range of Goss ware appeared and thrived. An agent was appointed for each town or locality, and he had the sole right to the sale of "Goss China" in that area.

In 1893 a new and successful range of coloured models of famous houses and other buildings was introduced, and over forty different models were produced in the range, product-ion of which continued until the last days of the firm.

William Henry Goss died in 1906, leaving a widow and seven children to mourn his passing. Whether they did so is a matter for conjecture, as he left Adolphus the sum of £4,000, while his works, his house, the business and its goodwill fell jointly to his sons Victor Henry and William Huntley Goss, together with the responsibility for caring financially for his widow. To his daughter, Eva Adeline, he left all his Stocks and Shares, together with a sum of £1,000 and all his household furniture and effects. And to his other two daughters, Edith Mountford and Florence Goss, he left sums of £1,000 each.

Heraldic China was by now firmly established, and rival firms were beginning to spring up, both at home and abroad. In 1912, the "Pottery Gazette" somewhat eulogistically described Goss as "something like a national benefactor in providing a number of artistic and not too expensive presents".

Finding the £4,000 for Adolphus Goss put a very great strain on the firm, and it was just beginning to re-establish itself when, in 1913, Victor Goss (who had replaced Adolphus as the firm's travelling salesman) was thrown from his horse and killed. This loss, together with the outbreak of War in 1914 marks the beginning of the decline of the firm, which continued under the supervision of William Huntley Goss. Labour shortages, the loss of overseas markets and changing public taste all weakened the firm's financial position, and efforts were made to improve the situation by the introduction of the various "Flags of the Allies" decorations, together with a model tank, bombs, shells, and a mine. This period also saw the introduction of a whole series of decorations depicting Regimental Badges and Warships' Crests, which, together with Arms of towns in France and Belgium where our troops were stationed, must have done much to tide the firm over this difficult period. For a few months, probably in 1918, a range of dolls' heads were produced, normal Continental sources no longer being available. This subject is dealt with more fully in the "Price Guide to Goss China" (page 182).

Various attempts were made during the 1920's to revive the firm's fortunes, and new models and decorations were introduced until the final days. In 1928, bankruptcy was imminent, and in the following year the firm was sold to George Jones and Sons Ltd., who had already acquired several of the other "heraldic porcelain" firms, including Arcadian, Swan, and Crescent. Trading as "W.H. Goss Ltd." (and later as "The Goss China Company Ltd.") they continued to produce wares bearing the Goss trade-mark, usually with the addition of the word "England", although many of these were made from Non-Goss moulds, and others were completely new lines. Of these, probably the most attractive, and certainly most sought-after by present-day collectors is the range of "flower girls", similar in style to their Doulton and Coalport counterparts.

What makes the work of the Goss factory so interesting to collectors is the limited range of some 700 models produced, all being named and ranging through historical and archaeological subjects, buildings, towers, light-houses, shoes, animals, etc. Also, of course, since the life of the factory was comparatively short, compared with say, Doulton, Wedgwood, or Copeland, it is possible to acquire specimens of each of the types of product of the firm.

'Theme collecting' is proving popular with these collectors who do not wish for, or cannot afford a rull range of Goss-ware. For instance, the cottages, of which there are some 48 basic models make a most attractive 'show'. The cheapest can still be bought for around £60 although the rarest now fetch many hundreds of pounds.

Parian busts are somewhat scarcer, and are rarely seen for sale. No collector should, however, be without a bust of "The Man" himself, produced in 1906 in sufficient quantity, and attractively priced (then!) at two shillings and sixpence, to enable even the most impecunious collector to acquire one as the centre-piece to the collection.

The Manufacture and Decoration of Goss China

Many people will not be aware of the fact that items of Goss China were made individually by hand with the aid of plaster-of-paris moulds — never by machinery or even on a potter's wheel.

The original models from which the plaster-of-paris moulds were produced were hand-made from blocks of ball clay, a darker and much more plastic substance than the china clay used to make the actual wares. These original models were made from detailed drawings (and latterly from photographs). Such was the degree of accuracy required that it is reported that 'The Cat and Fiddle Inn' at Buxton was actually visited in 1925, and exact measurements taken and colourings noted. A number of the earlier models of archaeological interest were made from scale drawings in contemporary literature, particularly Llewellyn Jewitt's 'Ceramic Art in Great Britain', published in 1878. Checking, where deemed advisable, was normally carried out by Adolphus Goss, and appropriate adjustments made when considered necessary. If a building was altered or re-decorated, then these amendments were faithfully reproduced by the factory. Perhaps the most notable cases of this are the First and Last House in England and Shakespeare's House.

It is regrettable that certain museums have labelled items incorrectly, probably the most interesting example to Goss collectors being in the Salisbury Museum where, for many years, the label of the Salisbury or Old Sarum Kettle was wrongly attached to a North African oil jar with two spouts and a central handle. This incorrect identification has been perpetuated in thousands of Goss models! This, together with the recent disclosure about the 'Carlisle Salt Pot' (which really had another use) may well give us cause for thought!

From the master-model in ball clay, a first plaster-of-paris mould was made, being in an appropriate number of sections — ranging from two in the case of a simple 'pot', to considerably more in the case of busts, statuettes, cottages, etc. This resultant mould was known as the 'block' or female, and from each of these a male or 'case' mould was made. Actual working moulds were then made from these 'case' moulds, ensuring that the mould had been suitably sized with soft soap dissolved in water to prevent sticking. While plaster-of-paris was used for these moulds on account of its facility in working and its great ability to absorb water, it had the disadvantage that, by constant wetting, it was liable to deteriorate and become rotten, (which would account, of course, for some models appearing in greater detail than others.)

The raw materials from which the final models were made were (a) for terra-cotta — Cornish clay, sand, ground glass, china stone, flint, sodium ash and sodium silicate, and (b) for the more widely-known parian or ivory-porcelain body, felspar either from Norway or Sweden, white glass (obtained by grinding up old bottles made of clear white glass), flints and kaolin china clay obtained from Cornwall.

(It may be appropriate to note here that the word Parian applies to the substance of the porcelain body itself whether left unglazed, glazed, or otherwise decorated. The use of the word solely with regard to unglazed wares is incorrect, and should therefore be discouraged.)

The foregoing materials were mixed with water, screened for dirt or lumps, and a large magnet used for the removal as far as possible of all iron fragments — the cause of the little 'spots' appearing in some of the earlier wares. The resultant liquid, of the consistency of thin cream, and known as 'slip', was poured into the various moulds until they were full. After a pre-determined time, all the surplus 'slip' was poured off, leaving an appropriately-thick coating inside the mould. This 'coating' was left until, by gradual absorption of water by the plaster-of-paris, it became sufficiently 'set' to be removed from the mould.

At this stage, seams, mould-marks and any other surplus pieces were removed, and handles, spouts, pedestals, together with any other items not from the first mould, would be added, using 'slip' as an adhesive. The complete piece was then known as 'green ware', and it was at this stage that any impressed marking was made on the model, i.e. the 'W.H. Goss', copyright details, or identification of busts.

The 'green ware' was now ready for its first or 'biscuit' firing, a critical process taking some five or six days, and involving a gradual rise in temperature to between 1,000 and 1,200 degrees centigrade, followed by a cooling-down period of some three days. In all, about seventeen to twenty-two tons of coal were required for this process, and it was obviously necessary, from an economic point of view, to fire as many models as possible at the same time, and an oven was normally packed with several thousand items for the one firing. Shrinkage during this firing could have been as much as one-sixth, and it will be appreciated that this would cause considerable problems when a piece of statuary or a group was being made from several separate moulds.

After this 'biscuit' firing, all items were examined, and, where necessary, cleaned by sand-paper, or, later, by machinery.

When satisfactory, the pieces which would be required for future glazing and/or decoration, were stored in the 'biscuit warehouse'. While there, the famous Goshawk trade-mark, together with any required descriptive matter, was printed on the pieces by means of transfers, or sometimes by a rubber die first pressed on an inked flannel pad.

All pieces for glazing were then passed to the 'dipping house', where they were dipped into vats of cold glaze, care being taken that it was spread evenly over the whole piece. After this, the pieces were placed on shelves near a stove, to dry the glaze prior to further firing. The materials used for the glaze comprised flint, china clay, whitening or carbonate of lime, Cornish stone, boracic acid, tincal, borax, carbonate of lead or oxide of lead, carbonate of soda, potash and felspar. These ingredients were heated in a small oven until they had all fused together, after which the mixture so obtained was ground to a powder and mixed with water.

In the glazing, or 'glost' ovens, the porcelain was fired for between sixteen and twenty-four hours, being raised to a temperature of between 1,000 and 1,050 degrees centigrade. Again, it was necessary to allow one or two days for the kiln to cool sufficiently before removing the contents. These were then sent to the 'sorting warehouse' for cleaning and examination for defects. All satisfactory pieces were put together, according to shape, until the contents of the oven had been exhausted. It was at this stage that all roughnesses of the glaze were removed and any blemishes left from the firing process were cleaned off or chipped away. The wares were then divided into three categories : (a) 'first', (b) 'seconds', that is wares having some slight defect, and (c) 'lump', i.e. those pieces which were cracked or whose defects were so serious that they could not be considered as 'seconds'. In some cases, however, an intermediate classification known as 'thirds' was made. All defective wares were re-classified to show where the defects originated, and the responsible parties were then called in to see the result of their inattention, lack of skill, or carelessness.

In the sorting warehouse the various models were kept in separate bins or pans, pending receipt of an appropriate order. When this was received, a sufficient quantity of the required model was taken to the printing shop where the desired design was put on each item. The printer had over seven hundred copper plates, each with up to twenty-four heraldic designs, mottoes, pictures, or other motifs engraved on them. He would heat the required plate and, using a flexible knife, put the appropriate coloured ink, usually black, but sometimes brown, red, blue or green, onto the appropriate part of the plate. The surplus ink was then scraped off and the plate polished with a velvet pad before being inserted into the 'bed' of the printing press. A tissue-paper 'transfer' was produced by passing the paper through the rollers together with the copper plate. The transfer was then dried, cut to shape, and passed to the transferer, who applied it to the appropriate place on the ware. Great care was taken over this process, especially where the transfer was being applied to fluted or embossed wares to ensure that the pattern was pressed right into all the crevices. The tissue-paper would normally remain until the end of the day's work, and was then carefully removed.

Pieces were then passed on to the enamellers to have the appropriate colours and gilding applied. Each enameller was allocated an individual mark which would normally be painted on the base of the model, using one of the colours of the decoration of that item. There is no evidence to support the story that enamellers' marks were regularly changed round, indeed an enameller would appear to retain her mark for the entire period of her work in that department. Whether or not a mark was 'handed down' to a later employee cannot be confirmed. Certainly the mark 'φ' was used for a very considerable number of years, but this may merely indicate that it was the mark of a particularly long-serving enameller.

After being coloured, the wares were then fired in the enamelling kilns which, being small, took only some five to nine hours for the firing process, the temperature required being between 900 and 1,000 degrees centigrade. Usually the fireman in charge of the enamel kilns tried to arrange for the fires to be drawn at about 5 p.m. so that they could be opened up about noon on the following day, and the wares could then be safely extracted.

After firing in the enamelling kilns, all wares were taken back to the enamel warehouse where they were checked for accuracy of colouring and for warping. If satisfactory, they were wrapped individually in tissue-paper before being passed to the packers who made up the individual orders, placing them in appropriate-sized casks and packed carefully in specially made wood wool. Unsatisfactory items were, however, returned to the individual enamellers (identifiable by their 'marks') so that mistakes or omissions could, where possible, be rectified.

Obviously unglazed items such as busts, figures and groups would only go through the early process, while monochrome transfer prints and decorations would not go forward to the enamellers, but would be passed straight through for firing. 'Hand-painted' wares would by-pass the 'transfer' stage, and the enamellers would work free-hand, often using designs from the Goss Pattern Books. Toby-jugs, Flower-girls and other multi-coloured items would be treated similarly.

It will be appreciated that the foregoing is only a brief summary of the whole process of manufacture and decoration as it was carried out in the Goss factory. Readers wishing for greater details are recommended to consult the appropriate literature in the reference section of their Public Library.

An interesting insight into the Goss factory at the turn of the century may be gleaned from John Galpin's interview with Laura Schofield, (who worked in the factory from 1897 until 1909) and which is reproduced under the title, 'A Long Look Back Into The Past' in 'Goss For Collectors' by John D. Magee, available from Milestone Publications.

Section A

Arms

A. Geographical Place Names

This section on Geographical place names contains approximately 3,500 different entries and this is not only by far the largest section in the book, but covers half the range of arms and decorations produced by the factory.

Thus it may be seen that the backbone of the Goss factory's trade was in supplying local arms to agents in almost every town, for sale as souvenirs on a massive scale. William Henry Goss' son Adolphus (and subsequently Victor), were the travellers for the firm and journeyed around the country selecting and appointing agencies, showing their samples, and taking orders. The firm's policy was to appoint one agent in each town so that there would be no competition in a particular area. The appointed agent would therefore stock a range of arms to include all the local villages, boroughs, town seals, counties and councils.

Many of the arms listed in this section only appear on later Goss England items. It is impossible to separate these from the earlier designs and so they have been included for completeness.
Note: A list of all the agents and their premises will be found in the Goss Record — reprinted and available from Milestone Publications.

Registered Number 77966

Readers will note that the above registered number appears in brackets after a number of place-names in the ensuing sections.

This registered number does **not** apply to the central **shield** or other motif applying to the town, but only to the design **surrounding** the shield, namely a beaded ring with scrolled pattern enclosing a red beaded shape on a blue ground.

This decoration should not therefore be referred to as a 'seal', as it is only an enhancement devised by the firm to make an otherwise rather plain coat-of-arms appear more attractive.

Seals proper will be referred to as such in these lists.

The following are all the examples known at present.

77966
Arundel
Brighton
Bridlington
Bridlington Priory
Calne
Dorothy Vernon
Dunmow Priory
Guildford
Hoylake & W. Kirby
Huddersfield
Ilkley
Newport, Mon
Newquay
Paignton
Petersfield
Portobello
St. Asaph
Southport
South Shields
Torrington
Totnes
Winchester College Quincentenary (1393-1893)

The last item is worth + £30.00; the remainder are of no extra value.

The value of the arms contained in this section is taken as the norm for the pricing of arms and decorations to be found in other sections.

Whilst some of the arms listed in this section are rare they would not be worth any more than more common examples. Therefore the prices in 'The Price Guide To Goss China' by the same author, would apply for all items bearing arms found within this section, with the exception of Empire and Foreign arms, for which £2.00 –£8.00 should be added on small pieces.

Where there was no foreign agent, the arms of a particular town or county were stocked by Ritchie & Co., the Stoke-on-Trent agent.

Sometimes, several coats-of-arms are found on plates. Six on a plate of up to 150mm would add £30.00, and up to twelve on a plate of approximately 250mm would add £50.00

A piece with more than one coat-of-arms would not necessarily be worth more than an example with only one. Larger vases and jugs are usually found with two or sometimes three arms.

Occasionally, the arms of a Nobleman were used by his local town or village. Thus the same arms may appear with different wording beneath. Rarely, the name of a Nobleman's Castle can also be found used in this manner.

Abbots Bromley
Abbotsbury
Abbotsbury Castle See Nobility, Earl of Ilchester
Abbotsford, Arms of
Abbots Langley
Aberaman
Aberavon
Aberayron U.D.C.
Abercarn
Aberchirder
Aberchirder, Burgh of
Aberdare
Aberdeen
Aberdour (two versions)
Aberdovey (two versions)
Aberfan
Aberfeldy (three versions)
Aberford
Aberforth
Aberfoyle
Abergavenny
Abergavenny, Burgh of
Abergavenny, Seal of
Abergele (two versions)
Abergele and Pensarn, The Urban District Council of
Abergynon
Aberlady
Aberlour
Abermorddu
Abernethy
Aberpennar, Mountain Ash 1905 (two versions)
Abersoch
Abersoch (Badge of Prince Owen of Gwynedd)
Abersychan
Abertillery, Ancient Arms of
Abertillery, The U.D.C. of
Abertillery, Seal of the Urban District Council of
Aberystwyth
Aberystwyth, Ancient
Aberystwyth, Modern
Abingdon (two versions)
Abingdon, The Burgesses' Seal of
Accrington
Acle
Acle, The Manor of
Acocks Green
Acton (two versions)
Addingham
Addlestone
Adlington, Cheshire
Adlington, Lancs.
Agbrigg (See also Bellevue)
Aigburth
Ainsdale, Lancashire (two versions)
Airdrie
Airton

Albury (two versions)
Alcester
Alcester, The Town of
Aldborough
Aldbourne
Aldbrough
Aldeburgh
Alderley Edge
Aldermaston
Alderney (Channel Isles)
Aldershot
Aldershot, The Borough of
Aldershot, The City of
Alexandria, Scotland (three versions)
Alford, Arms of
Alford, Aberdeenshire
Alford, Aberdeenshire, The Arms of Forbes of
Alford, Lincs.
Alford U.D.C.
Alfraham
Alfreton
Alfriston
Allendale, Northumberland
Allerds, Old Manor of, including Burnham Beeches
Allerton
Allithwaite
Alloa
Allonby
Almondbury
Almondsbury
Alness
Alness, Seal of
Alnmouth
Alnmouth, Manor & Borough of
Alnwick (two versions)
Alresford, Hants.
Alsager U.D.C.
Alsager
Alston
Altarnum, Cornwall
Altofts, Yorkshire (two versions)
Alton, Hants.
Alton, Staffs.
Altrincham
Alum Bay, Isle of Wight (two versions)
Alva, Scotland
Alverstoke
Alyth 1483
Alyth, Burgh of
Amble, Northumberland (three versions)
Ambleside
Amersham (three versions)
Amesbury
Amlwch, Wales
Amlwch, Port
Ammanford (two versions)
Ampthill

Andover
Anglesey, Isle of
Anglesey, Isle of (Ancient)
Annan (two versions)
Annfield Plain (two versions)
Ansdell
Anstruther Easter
Anstruther Wester
Antrim
Appin, Scotland
Appleby, The Borough of
Appledore
Arbroath (two versions)
Ardelve
Ardersier
Ardglass
Ardglass, The Seal of
Ardingly
Ardrishaig (two versions)
Ardrossan
Ardsley
Arisaig, Scotland
Arklow, Ireland
Armagh
Armathwaite, Cumberland
Arnside (two versions)
Arrochar
Arundel (77966)
Ascot (two versions)
Ashbourne
Ashburton
Ashby
Ashby-de-la-Zouch
Ashford, Derbyshire
Ashford, Kent
Ashford, Middlesex (two versions)
Ashford-in-the-Water
Ashington
Ashington and Hirst
Ashover
Ashtead (two versions)
Ashton, Lancs.
Ashton Keynes
Ashton-upon-Mersey
Ashton-under-Lyne
Ashwater
Askerne Spa, Yorkshire
Askrigg, Yorkshire, The Seal of
Askrigg, Villae'De
Aspatria, Cumberland
Astbury
Astley
Aston Clinton
Aston Hall, The Holt of
Aston Manor
Atherton, The Urban District Council of
Athlone
Attleborough
Atwick, Manor of Bala
Auchterarder (two versions)

Auchtermuchty
Auchtyfardle, Scotland
Audlem
Aviemore, Scotland
Avoch, Scotland
Avonmouth (three versions)
Axbridge
Axbridge, Seal of
Axminster
Ayerst Hall
Aylesbury (two versions)
Aylestone, Leicestershire
Aylsham
Ayr
Ayrshire
Aysgarth, Yorkshire (two versions)
Ayton

Babbacombe
Bacton
Bacup
Bagshot, The Seal of
Baildon, Yorks. (two versions)
Bainbridge
Bakewell
Bala
Bala, Manor of
Balbriggan
Balcombe
Baldock (two versions)
Balham
Ballantrae, Scotland
Ballater, The Town Council of the Burgh of, 1901
Ballina
Ballinasloe (two versions)
Balloch
Bally Bofey
Ballycastle
Ballyclare
Ballymena
Ballymenagh
Ballymoney
Ballynahinch
Ballyshannon
Balmaclellan
Balquhidder (two versions)
Balsall Common (two versions)
Bamburgh
Bamford
Banavie, Inverness
Banbridge, Ireland
Banbury
Banchory (two versions)
Banchory, The Seal of the Burgh of
Bandon, Ireland
Banff, Burgh of (three versions)
Bangor, City of
Bangor, Caernarvonshire

Bangor, Co. Down
Bangor, Co. Down, Seal of
Bangor-on-Dee
Bankfoot
Bantry
Banwell
Bara
Barcombe
Bardney
Bardsea
Bargoed, Wales
Bargoed-am-Byth
Barking Town U.D.C.
Barmouth
Barnard Castle
Barnard Castle, The Seal of
Barnes, Manor of
Barnet
Barnetby, Lincs (two versions)
Barnoldswick, Yorks (two versions)
Barnsley
Barnstaple (two versions)
Barrow-in-Furness (two versions)
Barrow-on-Soar, Leics.
Barry (two versions)
Barry, The U.D.C. of, inc. Barry Island
Barry, U.D.C. including Barry Dock
Barry Island
Barry, Glamorgan
Barton
Barton-on-Humber (three versions)
Barwick-in-Elmet
Baschurch
Basford, Notts
Basingstoke
Basingstoke, The Borough of
Baslow
Bath
Bath, The City of
Batley
Battersea, The Borough of
Battle, The Town of
Bawtry
Beaconsfield (four versions)
Beaminster
Bearwood
Beauly, Scotland
Beaumaris
Beccles, Seal of
Beccles, Ancient Seal of
Beckenham
Beckermet, Cumberland
Beck Hole, Yorks (two versions)
Bedale (two versions)
Beddgelert (two versions)
Bedford
Bedford, Villa Bedfordiensis
Bedford, Ancient Arms of

Bedfordshire
Bedlington
Bedwas, Wales
Bedworth
Beeley
Beer (See Lord Clinton, under Nobility)
Beeston
Beeston Castle
Beetham
Beighton
Belfast (two versions)
Belford, Manor of
Bellevue and Agbrigg
Bellingham (Northumberland)
Bellshill
Belmont
Belper (two versions)
Bembridge, Isle of Wight
Benderloch, Argyll
Benenden
Benfleet
Benllech Bay, Anglesea (three versions)
Ben Rhydding
Benson-on-Thames
Bentham
Bere Alston
Bere Alston, The Manor of
Berehaven
Berkeley, Glos.
Berkhampsted
Berkshire
Berkswell (two versions)
Bermondsey, The Borough of
Berry Narbor, Devon
Bervie, Scotland (two versions)
Berwick-on-Tweed
Berwick-on-Tweed, Arms of (Early)
Berwick-on-Tweed, The Seal of
Betchworth
Bethesda, Wales
Bethnal Green, The Borough of
Bettws-y-Coed
Beverley
Bewdley
Bewdley, The Borough of
Bexhill (two versions)
Bexhill-on-Sea
Bexley
Bexley, Arms of
Bibury
Bicester (two versions)
Biddenden
Biddulph, Staffs
Bideford
Bidford-on-Avon
Biggar
Biggleswade
Billericay (two versions)

Billingborough
Billingshurst
Bilston
Bingham
Bingley, Yorks
Binton
Birchington (two versions)
Birkdale (two versions)
Birkenhead
Birkenshaw
Birmingham, The City of
Birmingham (Full Arms)
Birnam
Birr, Co. Offaly
Birtley
Birstall
Bishop Auckland
Bishop's Castle, Salop
Bishop's Lydeard, Somerset
Bishop's Stortford
Bishopstone
Bishop's Waltham (see also Waltham Palace)
Blackburn
Blackgang, Isle of Wight
Blackhill
Blackmore
Blackpool (two colour variations) These Arms often but by no means always appear on sub-standard items.
Blackwood
Blaenau Festiniog (two versions)
Blaenavon
Blagdon
Blair Atholl
Blairgowrie
Blairmore, Scotland
Blakeney, Norfolk (two versions)
Blanchland
Blandford Forum
Blankney, Lincs.
Blarney
Blarney Castle
Blaydon-on-Tyne (two versions)
Blenheim
Bletchingley
Blockley, Worcs.
Bloxham
Blundellsands (two versions)
Blyth (two versions)
Blythburgh
Blyton, Lincs.
Boat of Garten, Scotland
Boddam
Bodedern
Bodiam
Bodiam Castle
Bodmin (two versions)
Bognor

Bognor Regis
Bolesworth
Bollington, Cheshire
Bolsey
Bolsover, Derbyshire
Bolton
Bolton Abbey
Bolton Castle, Redmire 1397 AD
Bolton-le-Sands
Bolton-on-Dearne
Bonar Bridge, Scotland
Boncath, Wales
Bonchurch, Isle of Wight
Bo'ness (Abbreviation for Borrowstounness)
Bootle, Cumberland
Bootle, Lancs.
Bootle-Cumlinacre
Bordon
Borough Bridge
Borrowash
Borth
Borth-y-Gest
Boscastle
Boscombe (two versions)
Boston, The Borough of
Boston Spa
Bothwell
Botley
Bottesford
Bourne
Bourne End (three versions)
Bournemouth (two versions)
Bourton-on-the-Water
Bovey Tracey
Bovey Tracey, Manor of
Bovington
Bowes
Bowes Park
Bowmore, Scotland
Bowness
Bowness-on-Solway
Bowness-on-Windermere (three versions)
Boxford, Suffolk
Boyton
Brackley
Bracknell
Bradford
Bradford, The City of
Bradford-on-Avon, Wilts. (two versions)
Brading, Ancient Arms of
Brading, Seal of
Brading, The King's Town of
Bradninch
Bradwell
Bradworthy
Braemar, Scotland
Braintree, Essex (two versions)

Braithwaite
Bramber
Bramber, Manor of
Bramhall
Bramley
Brampton
Bramshill
Branderburgh (See Lossiemouth)
Brandesburton
Brandon
Branksome
Brassington
Brasted
Bratton, Wilts. (two versions)
Braunton
Bray, Co. Wicklow (Shamrocks & Crown)
Bray, Co. Wicklow (Mermaid)
Breaston
Brechin
Brechin, Seal of
Brecon
Breedon-on-the-Hill
Brenchley
Brentford
Brentford, County Town of Middlesex.
Brentwood
Brewood (two versions)
Brewood, The Manor of
Bricket Wood, Herts.
Bridgend
Bridge of Allan
Bridge of Earn, Perthshire (three versions)
Bridge of Weir, Renfrewshire
Bridge Rule
Bridgewater, Borough of
Bridgewater, The Ancient Seal of
Bridgnorth
Bridlington (77966)
Bridlington, The Borough of
Bridport
Brierley Hill
Brigg
Brighouse
Brighouse, The Manor of
Brightlingsea, The Cinque Port and Liberty of
Brighton (two versions)
Brighton (77966)
Brighton, The Seal of (Ton Deo Fidemus)
Brigstock
Brill
Brinklow
Bristol
Bristol, City of
Briton Ferry, Glam.
Brixham

Brixham (landing of Prince of Orange – 1688)
Brixham, The Seal of Corporation of Harbour & Market
Brixton
Broadbottom
Broad Clyst
Broadford, Skye
Broad Haven, Wales
Broadheath
Broadstairs
Broadstairs, Royal
Broadstone
Broadwater
Broadway (two versions)
Brockenhurst
Brockham Green
Brodick, Scotland
Bromborough, Cheshire
Bromley, Kent
Bromsgrove
Bromyard, The Urban District Council of
Brookwood, Surrey
Broomfield
Brora, Sutherland
Broseley, Salop
Brotherton
Brotton, Yorks
Brough
Broughton-in-Furness
Broughty Ferry (two versions)
Broxbourne, The Manor of
Broxburn, Scotland
Brumby and Frodingham, Lincs.
Brundall
Brynmawr (two versions)
Brynsiencyn
Bubwith, Yorks.
Buckden
Buckfastleigh (two versions)
Buckhurst Hill (three versions)
Buckie
Buckingham, The Borough of
Buckinghamshire
Buckland Monochorum
Buckley
Bude
Budleigh Salterton
Builth
Builth Wells
Bull Bay, Angelsea
Bundoran
Bungay
Burbage
Burford
Burgess Hill, Sussex
Burgh, Lincs.
Burgh Castle, Manor of
Burgh Castle, Suffolk
Burghead, Morayshire

Burghead, The Seal of
Burley-in-Wharfedale
Burneside
Burnham, Bucks (two versions)
Burnham, Somerset
Burnham Beeches (three versions)
Burnham Market
Burnham-on-Crouch
Burnham-on-Sea
Burnham Thorpe
Burnley
Burnsall
Burntisland (two versions)
Burry Port (four versions)
Burscough Bridge, Lancs.
Burslem
Burton (two versions)
Burton Agnes, Yorks.
Burton Joyce, Notts.
Burton Latimer, Northants
Burton on Stather
Burton-on-Trent
Burwash (two versions)
Bury
Bury St. Edmunds
Bury St. Edmunds (Wolf with St. Edmund's Head)
Bushey
Bushmills, Antrim
Buttermere
Buttershaw, Yorks.
Buxted
Buxton (three versions)
Buxton Spa
Byfleet
Byfleet, The Seal of

Cadishead
Cadoxton, Glams.
Caergeiliog
Caergwrle (two versions)
Caerleon
Caerphilly
Caerphilly, Seal of U.D.C. of
Caersws
Caerwys (two versions)
Caister
Caister-on-Sea, Norfolk
Caistor, Lincs. (two versions)
Caldbeck
Calder Bridge
Callander
Callington
Calne (77966)
Calstock (two versions)
Calverley
Cam
Camberley
Camberwell, The Borough of
Camberwell and Peckham
Camborne

Cambridge
Cambridge, Full Arms
Cambridgeshire
Cambuslang
Camelford
Camelon
Camillford, The Seal of
Campbeltown (two versions)
Campden
Cannock
Cannongate, Ancient Burgh of
Canterbury, City of
Canterton
Canvey Island, Essex
Canvey-on-Sea, Essex
Capel
Capel Glanrhyd
Cappoquin, Ireland
Carbis Bay
Cardiff, Full Arms
Cardiff, City of
Cardigan, The Borough of
Cardigan, Seal of (Modern)
Cardigan, Seal of (Reverse)
Cardigan
Carisbrooke
Carlisle, The City of
Carlisle, Ancient Arms of
Carlisle, Ancient & Modern
Carlisle, Modern
Carlow
Carlton, Yorks.
Carlton and Netherfield
Carluke
Carmarthen
Carmarthen II
Carnarvon I
Carnarvon II
Carnarvon, The Seal of (Reverse)
Carnarvonshire (or Caernarvonshire)
Carnforth
Carnforth, County Palatine of Lancashire
Carnoustie (two versions)
Carperby, Wensleydale
Carr Bridge
Carrick Castle
Carrickfergus, The Seal of
Carrick-on-Suir, Ireland
Carrog
Carshalton
Cartmel
Castle Bay
Castle Cary
Castle Combe
Castle Donington
Castle Douglas
Castleford
Castle Hedingham
Castle Kennedy
Castle Rising
Castle Rock

Castlerock
Castleton (three versions)
Castletown, Ireland
Castletown, Isle of Man
Caterham
Catford
Caton
Catterick
Causeway Head
Cavan (two versions)
Cavendish, Suffolk
Caversham (two versions)
Cawood
Cawsand
Cawthorne
Cefyn
Cefyn Mawr
Cefn-y-Bedd
Cemaes Bay (two versions)
Cemaes Bay, Manor of
Cerrig-Druidion
Chadwell Heath
Chagford (two versions)
Chailey
Chale, Isle of Wight (two versions)
Chalfont St. Giles
Chalfont St. Peter
Chalford
Chapel-Allerton (two versions)
Chapel-en-le-Frith (two versions)
Chapel-St. Leonards
Chapeltown
Chard (1570)
Charlton, Manor of
Charlbury
Charleville, Ireland
Charmouth
Charterhouse
Chasetown
Chatburn (two versions)
Chatham
Chatteris
Cheadle (three versions)
Cheadle Heath
Cheadle Hulme
Cheam
Cheddar
Cheeswring
Chelmsford
Chelsea, The Borough of
Cheltenham
Cheltenham, The Borough of
Chepstow
Cheriton
Chertsey
Chesham
Cheshire
Chester
Chester, The City of
Chesterfield
Chesterfield, The Seal of the Borough of

Chester-le-Street
Chesterton, Staffs.
Chichester
Chichester, The Seal of
Chiddingfold
Chigwell
Chilham
Chingford (three versions)
Chinnor, Oxon.
Chippenham
Chippenham, The Ancient
Arms of
Chipping Norton (1606)
Chipping Ongar
Chipping Sodbury, The Seal of
the Borough of, 1680
Chirk
Chirk, Manor of
Chirnside
Chislehurst
Chiswick
Chiswick, The Urban District
Council of
Cholsey
Chorley
Chorley Wood
Chorlton-cum-Hardy
Christchurch
Chudleigh (two versions)
Churchdown
Church Gresley
Church Stretton (three versions)
Cirencester
Clacton-on-Sea (two versions)
Clapham (three versions)
Clare, Suffolk
Clawton
Clay Cross
Clayton-le-Moors
Cleator Moor
Cleckheaton
Cleethorpes (three versions)
Cleeve Hill
Cleobury Mortimer
Cleve, Somerset
Clevedon
Cleveleys (See also Thornton)
Cley-next-the-Sea
Clifton
Clitheroe
Clones, U.D.C.
Clonmel (two versions)
Clovelly
Clowne
Clun
Clun, The Seal of
Clydach, Wales
Clydebank
Clynder, Scotland
Clyne and Brora, Scotland
Coalville, Leics. (three versions)

Coatbridge, Seal of the Burgh of
Cobham
Cockburnspath
Cockermouth (two versions)
Cockermouth Castle, See
builder – Wm. de Meschines
Cockington (two versions)
Codicote
Colchester (two versions, i.e.
with both white and green cross)
Colchester, Port of
Coldingham
Coldstream, The Seal of
Coleford (Forest of Dean)
Coleraine
Coleshill
Colinsburgh
Collieston
Collingham
Collingham Bridge
Colne, Lancs.
Colonsay
Coltishall
Colwall
Colwyn (Arms of Old)
Colwyn Bay
Colwyn Bay and Colwyn, U.D.C. of
Colyton
Combe Down
Combe Martin
Compstall
Comrie, Scotland
Congleton
Coningsby
Conisborough
Coniston
Connah's Quay
Connaught
Consett (three versions)
Conway
Cookham
Cookham-on-Thames (two
versions)
Cookstown, Ireland
Corbets Tay
Corbridge
Corby (two versions)
Corfe Castle
Cork
Cornwall
Corpach, Inverness
Corris (two versions)
Corsham
Corwen, Wales
Cotherstone
Cottenham Park, London S.W.
Ancient Manor of
Cottingham
Coulsdon
Coupar Angus, The Burgh of
Coventry (two versions)
Cowbridge
Cowdenbeath (two versions)

Cowes
Cowfold
Coxhoe, Co. Durham
Coxwold
Crackington Haven
Cradley Heath
Craigellachie
Crail
Cramlington
Cranbrook
Cranleigh (two versions)
Crantock
Crathie
Craven Arms
Crawford
Crawley
Crawley, Manor of
Crayford
Crediton
Creetown
Creswell (two versions)
Crewe
Crewkerne
Crewkerne, The Seal of
Criccieth
Crick
Crickhowell
Cricklade
Cricklewood
Crieff
Croft Spa
Cromarty
Cromer
Cromford
Crondall
Crook
Crosby
Crossgates
Crosshills (two versions)
Cross Keys
Crouch End
Crowborough (three versions)
Crowhurst
Crowle
Crownhill
Crowthorne
Croyde, Devon
Croydon
Cruden Bay (See Port Errol)
(also Seal of)
Crumlin
Crystal Palace
Cuckfield (two versions)
Cudworth (two versions)
Cullen, Scotland (The Seal of)
Cullercoats
Cullompton
Cullompton, The Manor of
Culter, Scotland (two versions)
Cumberland
Cumbrae

Cumnock
Cupar, Fife (two versions)
Cwmavon
Cwmbran
Cwmllynfell
Cynwyd

Dacre Banks
Dalbeattie
Dalkeith
Dalkey
Dalmally, Argyllshire
Dalmellington
Dalry-Glenkens, Kircudbrightshire
Danby
Danbury, Essex
Dane Bridge
Darfield
Darlington
Darnick
Dartford (four versions)
Dartmouth (three versions)
Darvel, Scotland
Darwen
Davenport
Daventry (three versions)
Dawley
Dawley Under
Dawlish
Deal
Dedham (two versions)
Deganwy (two versions)
Delabole, Cornwall
Delph, Yorks
Denbigh
Denbighshire
Denholme
Denny, Scotland, The Parish
Council of the Parish of, 1618-
1895
Dent, The Seal of
Denton
Deptford
Derby (four versions)
Derbyshire
Dervaig, Scotland
Derwentwater
Desborough (three versions)
Devil's Bridge
Devil's Dyke
Devizes
Devon
Devonport
Dewsbury
Diabaig-Torredon, Ross-shire
Didcot (two versions)
Didsbury
Dingwall, Seal of (two versions)
Dinnington
Dinting Vale, Glossop
Disley

Manor of Bovey Tracey

Paignton. An Example of the 77966 Registered Design.

Bath

Hambledon

City of Exeter

Teignmouth

Southampton – The shield also appears alone.

Hampshire

Bude

Cheddar

Bournemouth. Matching Arms on a Bournemouth Pine Cone.

City of London

Manor of St. Just

Boscastle

Hastings. Shown here on a Portland Lighthouse.

Kent

Diss
Ditchling
Docking, Norfolk
Dolgelley U.D.C. (three versions including Dolgellau)
Dollar, Scotland (two versions)
Donaghadee, Ireland (two versions)
Doncaster
Doncaster, County Borough of
Donegal
Donington
Donoch
Dorchester (Dorset)
Dore, Derbyshire
Dorking
Dornoch (two versions)
Dorset
Douglas, The Borough of
Douglas (Isle of Man)
Douglas (Isle of Man) The Ancient Arms of
Douglas (Lanark)
Douglas Hall
Doune, Scotland
Dovedale (two versions) (one, Manor of Thorpe)
Dover, The Town of
Dover, The Cinque Port of
Dover, "Ville et Portus"
Dover, The Seal of
Dovercourt
Dowlais
Down, County
Downderry
Downe (two versions)
Downham
Downham Market
Downpatrick, Co.Down
Downton
Drax, Yorks.
Draycott
Drayton
Driffield
Drighlington
Drogheda
Droitwich
Drummond
Drummore
Drumtochty
Drymen, Scotland
Dubkin
Dublin
Dublin, The Seal of
Dudley
Dudley, The Borough of
Dudley Hill
Dufftown, Seal of the Burgh of (two versions)
Dukinfield
Dulmain Bridge
Dulverton

Dumbarton
Dumfries
Dunbar (two versions)
Dunbeath
Dunblane
Dunchurch
Dundalk
Dundee
Dunfermline (four versions)
Dungannon
Dungarvan
Dunkeld
Dunkeld-Caledonia (two versions)
Dunoon
Duns, Scotland
Dunstable
Dunster (two versions)
Dunwich
Durham, The City of
Durham, Hatfield Hall
Durham, County of
Duris Non Frangor
Durrington
Dursley (two versions)
Dyffryn
Dymchurch, The Seal of
Dynevor
Dysart, The Seal of (two versions)
Dyserth (three versions)

Eaglescliffe
Ealing, The Borough of
Earlestown (two versions)
Earls Barton
Earlsferry
Earlsferry, The Seal of
Earls Heaton, Nettleton
Earls Heaton, St.Peter's Church
Earl Shilton
Easington
Easingwold
East Aberthaw
East Anglia
East Ardsley
East Boldon
Eastbourne (two versions)
East Budleigh
East Cowes
Eastdean
East Dereham
East Grinstead
East Ham (two versions)
East Hartlepool
Eastleigh (two versions)
East Linton (two versions)
East Looe
East Molesey
Eastnor, Herefordshire
East Retford
East Riding of Yorkshire
East Stonehouse

East Sussex County Council
Eastwood (two versions)
Ebbw Vale (two versions)
Eccles
Eccleshall
Eccleston
Edenbridge
Edgware
Edinburgh
Edinburgh, The City of
Edinburgh, The Ancient Burgh of Cannongate
Edington
Edmonton
Edmonton, The County of Middlesex
Edwinstowe
Edzell (three versions)
Egglestone
Egham
Egham 1889
Egremont, Cumberland
Egton Bridge
Elgin
Elgin, The City and Royal Burgh of
Elie, Scotland
Elland
Ellastone
Ellastone, The Manor of
Ellesmere
Ellesmere Port (two versions)
Ellistown
Ellon, Scotland, Burgh of (two versions)
Elloughton
Elsecar (two versions)
Elstree (two versions)
Eltham
Ely
Embleton
Enderby
Enfield
Enfield U.D.C. of
England
Englefield Green
Ennerdale Bridge
Ennis
Ennis, Borough of
Enniscorthy
Enniskillen (two versions, one marked 1612)
Epping (two versions)
Epsom (two versions)
Epworth
Erbistock, Wales
Erdington
Erith
Errol, Scotland
Escrick
Esher (two versions)

Esholt
Eskdale
Essex
Eston, The Urban District Council of, 1894
Eton
Ettington
Etwall
Evesham
Evesham, The Borough of
Ewell
Exeter, The City of
Exeter, The County of
Exeter, Badge of the City of
Exmouth
Eyam
Eye, (Suffolk)
Eyemouth (two versions)
Eynsham

Failsworth
Fairfield
Fairford
Fairlie, Ayrshire
Fakenham, Lancaster
Falkirk
Falkirk, Ancient
Falkirk, 1906
Falkland, Scotland
Falmouth
Fareham
Faringdon (two versions)
Farnborough, Hants.
Farnborough, Kent (two versions)
Farncombe
Farndon
Farnham (two versions)
Farnham Common
Farningham
Farnley
Farsley
Faversham
Faversham, The Borough of
Fawley, Hants.
Felixstowe (two versions)
Felixstowe U.D.C.
Felixstowe and Walton U.D.C.
Feltham
Fenny Stratford
Fenton, Staffs.
Fermoy
Ferndale (two versions)
Ferrybridge
Ferryhill, Co.Durham (two versions)
Ferryside
Festiniog
Fettercairn, Scotland (two versions)
Filey
Finchingfield, The Borough of
Finchley

Findhorn, Scotland
Finedon, Northants.
Finsbury
Finsbury Park
Fishguard
Flamborough
Fleet, Hants.
Fleetwood (two versions)
Flint
Flint, The Borough of
Flintshire
Flintshire County Council, The Seal of, 1889
Flintwick, Beds.
Flookborough, Lancs.
Flore
Fochabers
Folkestone
Folkestone, The Cinque Port of
Foots Cray
Fordingbridge
Fordoun, Scotland, Burgh of
Fordwich
Forest Hill
Forest Row (two versions)
Forfar
Forfar, The Royal Burgh of
Formby
Forres
Fort Augustus
Fortrose, Scotland
Fortrose and Rosemarkie
Fort William (two versions)
Fort William, The Seal of
Foulsham
Four Oaks, Warwickshire
Fowey
Framlingham
Frant
Fraserburgh
Freiston
Frensham
Freshwater, Isle of Wight
Freuchie
Friern Barnet
Frimley
Frimley Green
Frinton-on-Sea
Friockhelm, Scotland
Fritton, Norfolk Broads
Frisington, Cumberland
Frodsham
Frome
Fulham
Fulham, The Borough of
Fulneck
Furness Vale
Fyvie, Scotland

Gainford
Gainsborough (two versions)

Gairloch, Ross-shire
Galashiels (four versions)
Gallatown
Galston, The Town Council of the Burgh of
Galway
Garboldisham
Gardenstown (two versions)
Garelochhead (two versions)
Garforth
Gargrave
Garlieston
Garmouth
Garnant
Garreglefa
Garstang, Seal of the Town of, 1686
Garston
Garth
Garth, King William's Tower?
Garve
Gatehouse of Fleet
Gatehouse of Fleet, The Seal of the Burgh of
Gateshead
Gateshead-on-Tyne
Gatwick
Gerrards Cross
Gifford, Scotland
Gilberdyke
Gildersome
Gillingham, Dorset
Gillingham, Kent (two versions)
Gipsyville
Girvan
Girvan, The Seal of the Burgh of
Gisburn (three versions)
Glaisdale (two versions)
Glamorganshire
Glan Conway
Glandford Brigg (was Glamford Bridge, is now Brigg)
Glasgow
Glasgow City
Glastonbury
Glastonbury, Borough of
Glenarm
Glencoe
Glenelg, Inverness
Glenfarg
Glenkens, See Dalry
Glenluce
Glenridding
Glen Urquhart, Loch Ness
Glossop
Gloucester, Ancient
Gloucester, Modern (two versions)
Gloucestershire County Council
Glyn Ceiriog (three versions)
Glyndfrwy

Gnosall
Goathland, Yorks.
Godalming
Godmanchester
Godshill, Isle of Wight
Goff's Oak
Golcar, Yorks.
Golders Green
Golspie, Scotland
Goodwick, Wales
Goole
Gorey, Ireland
Goring-on-Sea
Goring-on-Thames (two versions)
Gorleston-on-Sea (four versions)
Gorseinon
Gorton
Gosberton
Gosforth
Gosport, Seal of
Gosport, Borough of
Goudhurst
Gourock
Govan, Scotland
Grange, Borrowdale
Grangemouth
Grange-over-Sands
Grantham
Grantham, The Borough of
Grantham, The Seal of
Grantown-on-Spey (two versions)
Grantshouse, Berwickshire
Grappenhall
Grasmere
Grassington (two versions)
Grassington, Ancient Arms of
Gravesend
Grays, Essex
Grayshott (two versions)
Great Ayton (two versions)
Great Baddow
Great Bedwyn
Great Brington
Great Britain and Ireland (Royal Arms)
Great Britian (Sic) linked with the Arms of Republique Française
Great Crosby (two versions)
Great Grimsby
Great Haywood
Great Helen, Isle of Man
Great Horton
Great Malvern (two versions)
Great Marlow
Great Missenden
Great Missenden, The Seal of
Great Ormsby (two versions)
Great Yarmouth
Greenfield, Yorks (two versions)
Greengates

Greenlaw
Greenock, "God Speed Greenock"
Greenodd
Greenwich, "Ancient"
Greenwich (two versions)
Greetland
Gresford
Gretna Green
Greystoke (two versions)
Greystones
Grimsby, The County Borough of
Grindleford (two versions)
Grindleford Bridge
Grindleton
Gringley-on-the-Hill
Groeslon
Groombridge
Grossbridge
Guernsey (Channel Islands)
Guildford (77966)
Guildford, Seal of
Guildford, Ancient
Guiseley
Gullane (three versions)
Gulval
Gulval, Manor of
Gunnislake (three versions)
Gurnard
Gwbert-on-Sea
Gwyddelwern
Gwydr

Hackney
Hackney, The Borough of
Haddenham
Haddington
Haddington, Seal of the Burgesses of
Hadfield
Hadleigh, Essex
Hadleigh, Suffolk
Hailsham (two versions)
Halesowen
Halesworth
Halesworth, The Ancient Manor of
Halifax (two versions)
Halifax, Seal of
Halmer-End
Halstead
Haltwhistle (four versions)
Halwill
Hambledon, Cradle of Cricket, 1750
Hambleton
Hamilton
Hammersmith
Hammersmith, The Borough of
Hampden
Hampshire

Hampstead
Hampstead, South
Hampstead, West
Hampton Court, Founded by Cardinal Wolsey
Hampton Wick
Handcross
Handforth
Handsworth (two versions)
Hanley
Hanley, The County Borough of
Hanwell, Middx. (two versions)
Happisburgh, Norfolk (two versions, one dated "May 1929")
Harborne (two versions)
Harefield
Harewood
Harlech
Harlesdon
Harleston (two versions)
Harlington
Harmby
Harpenden
Harrington
Harris
Harrogate
Harrow
Hartington, Derbyshire
Hartland (two versions)
Hartlepool
Hartlepool, The Seal of
Hartley Wintney, Hants (two versions)
Harwich
Haslemere
Haslingden
Hastings
Hastings, The Seal of – Obverse
Hastings, The Seal of – Reverse
Haswell, Co. Durham
Hatfield (See Marquis of Salisbury)
Hatfield, Herts.
Hatfield, Yorks.
Hatfield Hall, Durham
Hatherleigh
Hathersage (three versions)
Havant (two versions)
Haven Street
Haverfordwest
Haverhill
Havering-Atte-Bowre
Haverthwaite
Hawarden, The Seal of
Hawes (two versions)
Hawick (two versions)
Hawkhurst
Hawkshead (two versions, one stating, "The Early Home of Wordsworth the Poet")
Haworth (two versions)

Haxey
Hay
Hay Castle
Haydon Bridge
Hayes
Hayes Barton
Hayfield
Hayle (two versions)
Hayling Island (two versions)
Haywards Heath
Haywards Heath Urban District Council
Hazel Grove
Heacham
Headcorn
Headingley
Heathfield
Heath Hayes
Heaton
Heaton Morris
Hebburn
Hebden
Hebden Bridge
Heckington
Heckmondwycke (Heckmondwike)
Heddon
Hednesford
Hedon
Hele Bay
Helens Bay (two versions)
Helensburch
Hellifield
Hellingly
Helmsdale
Helmsley (See Earl of Faversham)
Helpringham
Helsby
Helston, The Borough of
Hemel Hempstead
Hemel Hempstead, The Corporation of (three versions)
Hemel Hempstead Urban District Council
Hemingbrough
Hemsworth
Hendon
Hendon Urban District Council of, including Golders Green
Henfield
Henley-in-Arden
Henley-on-Thames, Ancient
Henley-on-Thames, 1624
Hensea
Henwood
Hereford
Hereford, Ancient Arms of the City of
Hereford, The City of AD 1645 (two versions)
Herefordshire

Herne Bay (two versions)
Herne Hill (two versions)
Herrington, Co. Durham
Hersham
Herstmonceaux
Hertford
Hertford, The Ancient Seal of
Hertfordshire
Hessle, Yorks (two versions)
Hest Bank
Heston & Isleworth Urban District Council, Hounslow
Heston
Heswall (two versions)
Hexham
Hexham, The Manor of
Heysham (four versions)
Heysham, Seal of the U.D.C.
Heythorpe
Heywood
Higham Ferrers
Higham Ferrers, The Seal of
Highampton
Highams Park
High Barnet
Highbridge
Highcliffe-on-Sea
Highgate
High Lane
Highworth
High Wycombe (four versions)
Hildenborough (two versions)
Hillingdon
Hillswick, Shetland
Hinckley
Hinderwell
Hindhead
Hingham
Hinkley
Hipperholme
Hirst
Hitchin
Hitchin, Ancient Seal of Hertford
Hoddesdon
Hodnet
Hogsthorpe
Holbeach
Holbeck
Holborn
Holborn, The Borough of
Holcombe Brook
Hollingworth
Holme Cultram, Silloth
Holmes Chapel
Holmfirth
Holmrook
Holsworthy (See Earl of Stanhope)
Holt, Norfolk
Holt, Denbighshire
Holyhead (two versions)

Holywell
Holywood
Honiton
Hook
Hook Norton
Hope, Derbyshire
Hopeman, Morayshire
Horbury
Horden, Co. Durham
Horley
Horley, Ancient Manor of
Horncastle
Hornchurch (two versions)
Horndean
Horning (two versions)
Hornsea
Hornsea, Yorks.
Hornsey, Middx., The Borough of (two versions)
Hornsey
Horrabridge
Horsforth
Horsham
Horsmonden
Horwich
Houghton-le-Spring
Hounslow
Hove, "Floreat Hova" (two versions)
Howden
Howorth, Lancs.
Howth
Hoylake, The Seal of
Holylake and West Kirby (77966)
Hoyland, Yorks (two versions)
Hucclecote
Hucknall Torkard
Huddersfield (77966)
Hull
Hulland
Hulme End
Hungerford
Hunmanby, The Manor of
Hunslet
Hunstanton
Hunstanton St. Edmunds
Hunstanton Manor
Hunter's Inn
Huntingdon
Huntingdon, The Borough of
Huntingdonshire
Huntley (two versions)
Hurstpierpoint
Hurworth-on-Tees
Hutton Hudby
Huyton
Hyde
Hythe, Hants.
Hythe, Kent
Hythe, The Cinque Port of
Hythe (See also Sir John Moore)

Ibstock
Ickenham
Idle, Yorks.
Idridgehay
Ilam
Ilford, Essex (two versions)
Ilford, The Urban District Council of
Ilfracombe (two versions)
Ilkeston
Ilkley (77966)
Ilminster
Immingham
Ingleton
Ince-in-Makerfield
Ingatestone
Ingleton (three versions)
Ingrow
Inellan
Innerleithen
Insch, Scotland (two versions)
Instow
Instow, The Manor of
Inverary (two versions)
Invergordon (four versions)
Inverkeithing
Inverkeithing, Seal of
Inverness
Inverurie (two versions)
Inverurie, The Seal of
Iona
Iona (Arms of Duke of Argyll)
Ipstones
Ipswich (two versions)
Irby
Ireland, Arms of
Ireland, Badge of (first version)
Ireland, Badge of (second version)
Ireland, Crest of
Irlam
Ironbridge
Ironville
Irthlingborough (three versions)
Irvine, Scotland (four versions)
Islay, Argyllshire
Isle of Ely
Isle of Man (Blue circle with "Quocunque Jeceris Stabit")
Isle of Man, Manx Legs
Isle of Man, Ancient
Isles of Scilly (F.Alg.Dorrien-Smith-Lord, Proprietor of)
Isle of Sheppey
Isle of Wight (Ancient)
Isle of Wight (Modern)
Islington
Iver
Ivinghoe
Ivybridge

Jamestown

Jarrow
Jarrow-on-Tyne
Jedburgh
Jerantown, Scotland
Jersey, Channel Isles
Jesmond Dene
Johnstone, Scotland
Jordans

Kames, Argyllshire
Keadby
Kearsley
Keighley, Borough of (two versions)
Keith, Scotland. Burgh of
Kellybray
Kelsall
Kelso
Kelty
Kelvedon
Kemnay (two versions)
Kempston
Kendal (two versions)
Kendal, The Seal of
Kenmare
Kennack
Kensal Rise
Kensington
Kensington, The Borough of
Kent
Keresley
Keston
Keswick (two versions)
Kettering
Kew
Keynsham
Kibworth Beauchamp
Kidderminster
Kidsgrove
Kidwelly, The Borough of
Kidwelly, Wales
Kidwelly, Wales. The Seal of
Kidwelly, The Common Seal of the Borough of
Kilbride, West
Kilburn, Manor of
Kilburn, Yorkshire
Kilchattan Bay
Kilconquhar
Kilcreggan
Kildare, Ireland
Kildwick, Yorks.
Kilgerran
Kilham
Kilkee
Kilkeel, Ireland (two versions)
Kilkenny
Kilkhampton (two versions)
Killaloe
Killarney
Killin, Scotland
Killsyth
Kilmalcolm, Renfrew
Kilmarnock

Kilmun
Kilrush
Kilwinning
Kincardine O'Neil
Kineton
Kinghorn, Fife (three versions)
Kinghorn, Fife. The Seal of
Kingsbarns 1630 (two versions)
Kingsbridge (two versions)
Kingsbury, Piccadilly
Kingsdown
Kingskerswell
Kingskettle
Kingsley
Kings Lynn (two versions)
Kings Norton, The Manor of
Kingston
Kingston-on-Hull
Kingston-on-Spey
Kingston-upon-Thames, Seal,
Kingston-upon-Thames
Kingstown, (Dun Laoghaire) Ireland (two versions)
Kingswear
Kingswood
Kington
Kingussie, The Burgh of (three versions)
Kinlochleven (two versions)
Kinloch Bannoch (two versions)
Kinross
Kinsale (two versions)
Kintbury
Kintore
Kinver (two versions)
Kippax, Yorks.
Kippford
Kirby, Yorks.
Kirham (three versions)
Kirk Braddan
Kirkburton
Kirkby
Kirkby-Kendal, 1575
Kirkby Lonsdale
Kirkby Stephen
Kirkby Stephen, Pendragon Castle
Kirkcaldy
Kirkcudbright
Kirkcudbright, The Seal of
Kirkcudbrightshire
Kirkintilloch
Kirkmichael
Kirkmichael, Arran
Kirk Onchan, Isle of Man
Kirkoswald
Kirkstead
Kirkton
Kirkwall
Kirn
Kirriemuir
Kirton, 1250 A.D.

Knaresborough
Knaresborough, The Borough of
Knebworth
Knighton
Knighton, Radnor
Knott End
Knottingley
Knowle
Knutsford (origin - Canute's Ford) (two versions)
Kyleakin, Isle of Skye
Kyle of Lochalsh
Kyles of Bute

Laceby
Ladybank (two versions)
Laindon
Lairg, Sutherlandshire
Lamberhurst
Lambeth
Lambeth, The Metropolitan Borough of
Lamlash (two versions)
Lampeter
Lanark
Lancashire
Lancashire, The County Palatine of
Lancaster
Lancaster, County Palatine of
Lancaster, Duchy of
Lanchester
Landrake
Land's End (two versions)
Langford
Langholm Burgh
Langport
Langtree
Lanivet
Larbert
Largo
Largs
Larkhall (two versions)
Larne
Lartington
Lasswade
Lauder, Scotland (two versions)
Lauder, Seal of the Burgh of
Launceston
Laurencekirk, The Burgh of (three versions)
Laxey, Isle of Man (two versions)
Leatherhead
Leamington Spa, Royal
Leatherhead
Lechlade
Ledbury
Lee (two versions)
Lee-on-Sea (two versions)
Lee-on-the-Solent, Hants.
Leeds, The City of
Leek, Staffs.
Leicester

Leicester, The City of
Leicestershire
Leigh
Leigh, Lancs.
Leigh-on-Sea (two versions)
Leigh-on-Sea Urban District Council 1897
Leigh-on-Sea, incorporated with Southend 1913
Leighton Buzzard
Leinster
Leiston
Leith
Leith, Seal of
Lelant
Lenboxtown
Lent Rise, Burnham
Lenzie ("Ca' Canny but Ca' awa")
Leominster
Leominster, The Seal of
Lerwick (Orange Sky)
Lerwick (Yellow Sky)
Lerwick, Shetland Islands
Leslie, Scotland
Letchworth
Leven, Scotland, The Burgh of (two versions)
Leven, Scotland, The Seal of the Burgh of
Leven, Yorkshire
Levenshulme (three versions)
Lewdown
Lewes
Lewisham
Lewisham, The Borough of
Lewisham, including Sydenham
Leyburn (two versions)
Leyland
Leyton
Leyton, The Manor of
Leytonstone (three versions)
Lichfield, The City of
Lichfield, The Seal of the City, 1688 ('Commune civitatus')
Lickey Hills, The
Lidget Green
Lifton
Limavady (two versions)
Limekilns, Scotland
Limerick (three versions)
Limpsfield
Lincoln, Ancient Arms of
Lincoln, The City of
Lincolnshire
Lindfield
Lindisfarne, Holy Island
Lingfield
Linlithgow (three versions)
Linlithgow, Seal of the Royal Burgh of (Obverse)
Linlithgow, Seal of the Royal Burgh of (Reverse)

Linslade
Linslade Urban District Council
Linton
Liphook
Lisburn, Ireland
Liscard, Wallasey (three versions)
Liskeard
Little Eaton
Littlehampton
Littleport, Isle of Ely (two versions)
Littlestone-on-Sea
Little Sutton
Liverpool, Aintree
Liverpool, The City of
Liverton
Lizard, The
Llanarmon Dyffryn Ceiriog
Llanarth
Llanbedr
Llanbedrog (three versions)
Llanberis (two versions)
Llancefni
Llandaff
Llanddewi
Llanddulas (two versions)
Llandilo
Llandilo, The Borough Prescription
Llandiloes
Llandovery 1484
Llandovery, The Borough of
Llandrillo
Llandrindod Wells (two versions)
Llandudno
Llandudno Junction (two versions)
Llandwrog
Llandyssul
Llanelly (three versions)
Llanerchymedd
Llanfachraeth
Llanfaethin
Llanfair
Llanfair-Caereinion
Llanfair-Caereinion, The Manor of
Llanfairfechan
Llanfairpwllgwyngyllgogery-chwyrndrobwllttysiliogogogoch (two versions). This name is found in full around the brim of some Welsh hats.
Llanfair-Talhaiarn
Llanfyllin, The Borough of (two versions)
Llangammarch Wells
Llangattock
Llangefni
Llangerniow
Llangoed
Llangollen (three versions)
Llangarig, The Manor of

Llanhilleth
Llanidloes
Llanilar
Llanon
Llanrhaiadr yn Mochnant
Llanrhystyd
Llanrug (two versions)
Llanrwst
Llanstephan (two versions)
Llantrisant
Llantrisant Town Trust, 1889 (Matt. V XIV)
Llantwit Major
Llanwrtyd Wells (two versions)
Llanwnda (two versions)
Llanwrda
Llanybyther
Llanymynech
Llechryd
Loanhead
Lochalsh
Lochcarrow
Lochearnhead
Lochgelly
Lochgilphead
Lochgoilhead
Lochinver
Lochmaben, The Royal Burgh of (two versions)
Lochmaddy, North Uist
Lochransa
Lockerbie
Lockerbie, The Burgh of
Lockington
Lockwood
Loddon
Loftus-in-Cleveland
London, The City of
London County Council (Note: Arms not authentic)
Londonderry
Long Buckby
Long Eaton, The Seal of
Long Eaton, The Seal of the Urban District Council of
Long Itchington
Long Melford
Long Preston (two versions)
Longridge
Longsight
Longstone
Long Sutton (Holland, Lincs.)
Longton
Longton, The Seal of
Looe (being the joint Arms of East and West Looe)
Lossiemouth
Lossiemouth and Branderburgh
Lostwithiel
Loughborough
Loughborough, The Borough of

Loughton
Loughton ("Free of the Forest")
Louth
Louth, The Ancient Arms of
Lower Bebington
Lower Clatford
Lower Large, Fife
Lowestoft (Colour variations)
Lowestoft, The Seal of
Lowmoor
Luddenden Foot
Ludgershall (two versions)
Ludham
Ludlow (two versions)
Lulworth
Lulworth Cove
Lumphanan
Lundy Island
Lundy Isle, The Manor of
Luss
Lustleigh
Luton
Lutterworth
Lybster
Lydbrook, Forest of Dean
Lydd (two versions)
Lydford
Lydney, Forest of Dean
Lyme Regis
Lyme Regis, The Seal of
Lymington
Lymington, The Seal of
Lymm
Lympstone
Lyndhurst
Lyndhurst, in the New Forest
Lynmouth
Lynton
Lytham
Lytham St. Annes
Lythe

Mablethorpe (two versions)
Macclesfield (two versions)
Macduff (two versions)
Machrihanish, Argyllshire
Machynlleth
Machynlleth 1894
Madeley
Maentwrog, Mairionydd
Maesteg
Maesteg, Wales
Magherafelt, Ireland
Maida Vale
Maidenhead (two versions)
Maidenhead, The Seal of
Maiden Newton
Maidstone
Malahide
Maldens and Coombe Urban District Council, including New Malden
Maldon

Sunderland

Skegness

Uttoxeter

Blackpool

Seal of Kendal

Ilkley. An Example of the 77966 Registered Design.

City of Liverpool

A Trinket Tray Bearing the Arms of **The Duke of Norfolk, Yorkshire, Sheffield** and **The Cutlers Company, Sheffield.**

A Large Three Handled Loving Cup Depicting the Arms of **King Edward VII., Stoke Newington** and **Southwark.**

Mallaig, Scotland
Mallow
Malmesbury
Malpas, Cheshire
Malton (two versions)
Manchester
Manchester, Bellevue
Manningtree
Manorbier
Manor Park
Mansfield
Mansfield, The Borough of
Mansfield Woodhouse
Mappleton
Marazion
Marazion, Cornwall, The Seal of the Mayor and Borough of 1595 A.D.
March
March Town
Marchington
Marchwood
Marden
Marfleet (two versions)
Margate
Marhamchurch
Marianglas
Market Bosworth. The Battle of Bosworth Field, 22 Aug. 1485
Market Deeping
Market Drayton
Market Harborough
Market Lavington (two versions)
Market Rasen
Markinch
Markinch, The Provost, Magistrates & Councillors of the Burgh of
Marlborough
Marlborough, The Borough of
Marlow
Marple
Marple, The Urban District of
Marple Bridge
Marsden
Marsk
Marske-by-the-Sea (two versions)
Marston Green
Martham
Martham, St. Mary
Maryboro'
Maryborough
Maryport
Mary Tavy (two versions)
Masham
Matlock
Matlock, The Seal of
Matlock Bath
Matlock Bridge
Mauchline, Scotland
Maud, Aberdeenshire
Maxwelltown

Maybole
Mayfield (three versions)
Medon
Meigle
Melbourn, Cambridgeshire
Melcombe Regis (See also Weymouth)
Melcombe Regis, The Seal of
Meliden
Melksham
Melrose
Meltham
Melton, Suffolk
Melton Mowbray
Menai Bridge (two versions)
Menai Bridge Urban District Council, Seal of
Menston
Meole Brace, Shropshire
Meole, Lancashire
Meopham
Mere (two versions)
Merioneth
Merionethshire
Mersea
Merthyr Tydfil (three versions)
Messingham
Metheringham
Methil
Methley
Methlick
Methven
Methwold
Mevagissey
Mexborough (two versions)
Micklefield
Mickleover
Mid-Calder
Middlecot
Middleham Castle 1190 A.D.
Middleham Castle 1270 A.D.
Middlesborough (two versions)
Middlesex
Middlesex County Council
Middleton
Middleton-in-Teesdale (three versions)
Middleton-One-Row
Middleton St. George
Middlewich
Midhurst (two versions)
Midsomer Norton
Milborne Port (two versions)
Miles Platting, Manchester
Milford (two versions)
Milford, Staffs. (two versions)
Milford Haven (two versions)
Milford-on-Sea
Miller's Dale
Mill Hill
Millom

Millport, Burgh of
Milnathort, Scotland
Milnrow
Milnsbridge
Milnthorpe
Milton, Hants.
Milton Abbas
Milton Regis
Milverton
Minchinhampton
Minchinhampton, The Manor of
Minehead
Minehead, The Ancient Port of
Minstead - 'Ye Trusty Servant'
Minster (Actually the Arms of Marquise Conyngham)
Minster, The Seal of
Minsterley
Mirfield
Misterton (two versions)
Mistley
Mitcham
Mobberley
Modbury
Moffat (two versions)
Mold
Molesworth
Monaghan
Moniave, Scotland (two versions)
Monifieth, Scotland (two versions)
Monk Fryston
Monkseaton
Monkwearmouth
Monmouth
Monmouth, Arms of
Monmouth, The Seal of
Monmouthshire
Montgomery, Wales
Monton
Montrose (two versions)
Monymusk, Scotland
Morecambe
Moreton
Moretonhampstead (two versions)
Moreton-in-Marsh
Morley
Morpeth
Morthoe (two versions)
Mortimer
Mortimer Common
Mortlake
Morwenstow
Moseley, The Manor of
Moseley Village
Mossley
Motherwell
Motherwell, Burgh of
Mottram
Mountain Ash (See Aberpennar)
Mountnessing
Mousehole

Much Wenlock
Much Wenlock, The Borough Seal of
Muir-of-Ord
Mull
Mullingar
Mullingar, The Seal of
Mullion
Mumbles
Mundesley (two versions)
Munster
Murton, Co. Durham
Musselburgh (two versions)
Muswell Hill
Mytholmroyd

Naas, Ireland
Nafferton
Nailsworth
Nairn
Nannerch
Nanpean
Nantwich
Nantymoel
Narborough
Navan, Ireland
Navenby
Neath
Neath, The Seal of
Nelson, Lancs.
Neston, Cheshire
Nether Stowey
Nether Whitaker
Nethy Bridge
Nevin
Newark
Newark-upon-Trent
Newbiggin-by-the-Sea
New Bradwell
Newbridge
Newbridge (Mon.)
Newbridge-on-Wye
New Brighton
Newburgh
Newburn-on-Tyne
Newbury (Burgus Newberie)
Newbury, City of
Newby Bridge
Newcastle, Co. Down, Ireland
Newcastle Emlyn
Newcastle-on-Tyne (two versions)
Newcastleton
Newcastle-Under-Lyme
New Cross
New Deer, Aberdeenshire
Newent
New Ferry (two versions)
New Forest, The (King William II - Rufus) (two versions)
New Galloway
Newhall
Newhaven, Sussex (three versions)

New Holland
Newlyn (two versions)
Newlyn, The Manor of
New Maltby
Newmarket, Suffolk
Newmarket, Wales
New Mills
Newmilns
Newmilns and Greenholm
New Milton
New Milton, The Manor of
Newnham-on-Severn
New Pitaligo
Newport, Fife
Newport, Isle of Wight
Newport, Monmouthshire(77966)
Newport, Pembrokeshire
Newport, Pembrokeshire, The
Seal of
Newport, Shropshire
Newport-on-Tay
Newport Pagnell (two versions)
Newquay
Newquay (77966)
Newquay, Cardiganshire
Newquay, Co. Cardigan
Newquay Llandyssul, Wales
New Radnor
New Romney
New Romney, The Cinque
Port of
New Ross
Newry
Newton Abbot
Newton Abbot, Wolborough
Highweek
Newtonards 1613
Newton Heath
Newton-le-Willows (two versions)
Newtonmore
Newton Stewart, Wigtownshire
Newtown, Wales, The Seal of
Newtown (N.Wales)
Newtownards, Co.Down
Neyland, Wales
Neyland, The Manor of
Niton
Norbreck
Norfolk
Normanton 1895
Northallerton
Northam
Northampton
Northampton, The Mayor's
Official Seal
Northamptonshire
North Berwick
North Cave
North Ferriby
Northfleet
Northfleet Urban District
Council
Northiam

North Mildenhall
Northop
North Queensferry
North Tamerton
North Tawton
North Shields
North Shields and County
Borough of Tynemouth
North Somercoats
Northumbria
North Walsham
Northwich
Northwood (See also Ruislip)
Norton Fitzwarren
Norton-on-Tees
Norwich
Norwich, City of
Norwood
Noss Mayo
Nottingham, The City of (two
varieties – differing supporters)
Nottingham, The City of 1887
1909
Nottinghamshire
Novar, Scotland
Nuneaton, The Borough of (Seal)

Oakamoor
Oakengates, Salop(three versions)
Oakham
Oaktree Alexandria
Oakworth
Oban (two varieties)
Odiham
Ogilvy
Okehampton (two versions)
Old Charlton
Old Colwyn U.D.C. (see Colwyn)
Old Deer
Old Deer Village, Scotland
Oldham
Old Laxey
Old Meldrum
Ollaberry, Shetland
Ollerton
Olney
Omagh, Ireland
Ongar (three versions, one being
a colour pictorial of a fox.)
Openshaw
Orford
Orkney, The County of
Ormskirk (two versions)
Orpington
Osmotherley
Ossett
Oswestry
Oswestry, Seal of
Otley (two versions)
Otford
Ottery St.Mary (See John de
Grandisson)

Oulton Broad, Suffolk Broads
Outwell
Ovenden
Overstrand, Norfolk (two
versions)
Overton-on-Dee
Owston Ferry
Oxford
Oxford, The City of
Oxford, Arms of the City of
(Full Arms)
Oxshott, 1889
Oxted
Oyne
Oystermouth

Paddington
Paddington, The Borough of
Padstow
Paignton (77966)
Painswick
Painswick - Motto "Bow-Wow"
Paisley (two versions)
Paisley, The Seal of the
Borough of
Palling-on-Sea
Pangbourne (two versions)
Parkgate
Parkstone (two versions)
Partick
Partridge Green
Parwich
Pateley Bridge (two versions)
Patrick
Patrington, Yorks.(two versions)
Patterby Bridge
Patterdale
Paull, Yorks.
Peacehaven (two versions)
Peak Forest
Peckham (See Camberwell)
Peebles
Peel, The City of
Peel, The Seal of
Pegwell Bay
Pelton Fell
Pemberton
Pembrey
Pembroke
Pembroke,The County of
Pembroke Dock
Pembury
Penarth
Pencader
Pendragon Castle (See Kirkby
Stephen)
Pendine (two versions)
Pendleton
Penicuik, Scotland (two versions)
Penistone
Penkridge

Penmaenmawr
Penrhiwceiber
Penrhyn Bay
Penrhyn
Penrhyndeudraeth
Penrhyndeudraeth, The Manor
Penrith
Penryn
Penryn-side
Pensans A.D. (See Penzance)
Penshurst
Pensilva
Pentowan
Pentraeth
Pentre
Penzance, The Borough of, 1614
Penzance (Seal)
Peplow
Perran
Perranporth (or Perran-Porth)
Perth
Perthshire
Peterborough,The City of
Peterborough,The City and
Borough of
Peterborough,The Borough of
Peterhead (two versions)
Petersfield (77966)
Petworth
Pevensey
Pewsey
Pickering
Pickering, The Duchy of
Lancaster
Pill, Somerset (two versions)
Pinchbeck
Pinhoe
Pinner
Pinxton, Manor of
Pirn Mill
Pitlochry
Pitsea
Pittenweem
Plockton
Plymouth
Plymouth, The City of
Plymouth (Full Arms)
Plympton
Plympton, The Seal of the
Borough of
Pocklington
Polegate
Polperro (two versions)
Polzeath
Pontardulais
Pontefract, The Arms of, 1558
Pontrhythallt
Pontyclun
Pontycymmer
Pontypool (two versions)
Pontypool (The Manor of)

Pontypridd
Pont y Rhyd, Llangoed
Poole
Poole, including Parkstone
Poolewe
Pooley Bridge
Poplar
Poplar, The Borough of
Porlock
Porta Vacat Culpa (See Repton Town & School)
Portadown, Ireland
Portadown, Town Commissioners 1883
Portaferry, Ireland
Portarlington
Portbury, The Ancient Manor of
Portchester, The Manor of
Port Ellen, Islay, Argyllshire
Port Erin (four versions)
Port Erroll (See also Cruden Bay) (three versions)
Port Gavern
Porth (two versions)
Porthcawl (four versions)
Porthleven
Port Isaac
Portishead
Portland
Portland, The Island and Royal Manor of
Portland, Dorset, The Island and Royal Manor of Portland Urban District Council
Port Logan, Wigtonshire
Portmadoc (Ynyscynhaiarn)
Portobello (77966)
Portpatrick (three versions)
Portreath
Portree, Skye
Portrush (two versions)
Port St.Mary (two versions)
Port St.Mary's Commissioners
Portscathe
Portsea
Portslade-by-Sea
Portsmouth
Portsmouth, City of ("Heaven's Light Our Guide")
Portsmouth (with fabricated Arms of Southsea)
Portsoy, The Burgh of
Portsoy, The Seal of the Burgh of
Port Stewart
Port Sunlight (three versions)
Port Talbot (two versions)
Port William
Potter Heigham
Potter's Bar

Potton
Potton, The Manor of
Poulton-le-Fylde (two versions)
Powfoot
Poynton
Prees, Salop.
Preeseweene, Rhoswriel
Prees Heath
Prescot, Lancs.
Prestatyn (three versions)
Prestbury (two versions)
Presteign
Preston
Preston Paignton
Prestonpans, The Burgh of, 1893 A.D.
Prestwich
Prestwick
Princes Risborough
Princetown (three versions)
Prittlewell
Prudhoe-on-Tyne
Pudsey
Pulborough (two versions)
Purfleet
Purley
Purley, Surrey
Purley, in the Rural District of Croydon
Putney, The Borough Arms of
Putney (See also Wandsworth)
Pwllheli
Pwllheli, The Seal of
Pyecombe

Quainton
Quarndon
Queenborough
Queensbury
Queensferry (See also South Queensferry)
Queenstown (Cobh)
Quorn

Raby Castle
Radcliffe
Radcliffe-on-Trent
Radlett (two versions)
Radlett, The Manor of
Radnor
Radnorshire
Radstock
Raglan
Rainford
Ramsbottom
Ramsey, Huntingdon
Ramsey, Isle of Man
Ramsgate
Randalstown
Rathmullen
Raunds, Northants

Ravenglass (two versions)
Ravensthorpe
Ravenstonedale
Rawcliffe
Rawmarsh and Parkgate
Rawtenstall
Rayleigh, Essex
Rayleigh, The Parish of
Reading
Reading, The Borough of
Redbrook, Monmouthshire
Redcar
Redcar, The Borough of
Reddish
Redditch
Redesdale (The Royal Artillery)
Redhill
Redhill (as Reigate)
Redruth
Red Wharf Bay, Anglesea
Reedham
Reeth
Reigate (Arms repeat of Redhill)
Renfrew, The Burgh of
Repton Town - Motto "Porta Vacat Culpa".
Reston
Retford
Retford, The Seal of
Rhayader
Rhosllanerchrugog
Rhosllanerchrugog, The Arms of Wales
Rhosneigr
Rhos-on-Sea (three versions)
Rhuddlan, The Manor of
Rhyd-ddu
Rhydymwyn
Rhyl
Riccall
Richmond, Surrey
Richmond, Surrey, the Borough of
Richmond, Yorkshire
Rickmansworth
Riddings
Riddlesdown
Riddlesdown, The Seal of
Ridley Hall
Rilla Mill
Rillington
Ringmer
Ringwood (two versions)
Ripley, Derbyshire (two versions)
Ripley, Yorks (West-Riding)
Ripon
Ripon, The Festival 1896
Ripponden
Risem
Righten

Robertsbridge
Robin Hood's Bay
Robin Hood's Bay, the Manor of
Rochdale
Rochdale, The Borough of
Roche, Cornwall
Rochester
Rochester, The City of
Rochford
Rochford, The Manor of
Rochford, the Urban District Council of, including Hockley
Rock Ferry (three versions)
Rodley
Rodney Stoke
Roker
Rolvenden
Romford, the R.D.C., including Upminster
Romford, The Seal of the Manor of Havering atte Bowre
Romiley
Romsey
Romsey, The Seal of, 1578
Rosehearty (two versions)
Rosemarkie
Rosemarkie (See also Fortrose)
Roslin
Rosneath (The Duke of Argyll)
Rossett (two versions)
Rosslare
Rosslyn
Ross-on-Wye (three versions)
Rosthwaite, Borrowdale
Rostrevor, Co.Down
Rosyth (two versions)
Rothbury
Rotherfield
Rotherham
Rothes
Rothes, The Seal of
Rothesay, the Royal Burgh of (two versions)
Rothley
Rothwell
Rottingdean
Roundhay
Row, Scotland
Rowsley (two versions)
Roydon
Royston, Herts. (four versions)
Royston, Yorks.
Royton
Ruabon
Ruan Minor
Ruddington
Rudyard, Yorks.
Rugby (two versions)
Rugeley
Ruislip

City of St. Andrews

Seal of Fort William

St. Mary's, Isles of Scilly

Sercq (Sark)

Oban

Queenborough

Alderney

Jersey (Guernsey similar)

Sheppey

Dublin

Frinton-on-Sea

Norwich. An Early Crest named on the base of the model.

Minster

Bray, Ireland

See of Worcester

City of Peel

31

Ruislip, Northwood
Runcorn (two versions)
Runswick Bay (three versions)
Runton, the Manor of
Rushden (two versions)
Rusholme, the Manor of
Ruskington
Russington
Ruswarp
Rutherglen
Ruthin
Ruthin, The Mayor, Aldermen and Burgesses of
Rutland, the County of
Ruyton (XI Towns)
Ryde (two versions)
Rye, Cinque Port of
Rye, The Seal of
Rye, the Seal of (with Legend of Rye)
Ryton-on-Tyne

Saffron Walden
St. Abbs
St. Agnes
St. Albans
St. Albans, City of
St. Andrews
St. Andrews, City of
St. Annes-on-Sea
St. Annes-on-the-Sea
St. Ann's Chapel
St. Asaph (77966)
St. Austell
St. Bees
St. Blaise, A.D.516
St. Blazey
St. Blazey, the Manor of
St. Boswells
St. Breward
St. Buryan
St. Buryan and Lamorna
St. Catherines
St. Clears, the Ancient Seal of the Corporation of
St. Cleer
St. Columb, 1638
St. Columb Major
St. Columb Minor
St. Columba
St. Crantock
St. Davids
St. Dennis
St. Dogmaels
St. Fergus
St. Fillans
St. Helens, Isle of Wight
St. Helens, Lancs.
St. Ives, Cornwall
St. Ives, Cornwall, the Seal of
St. Ives, Huntingdonshire

St. Johns, Isle of Man
St. Just, Cornwall
St. Just, the Manor of
St. Lawrence
St. Leonards
St. Margarets-at-Cliffe
St. Margaret's Bay
St. Margaret's Hope, Orkney
St. Martins
St. Marychurch
St. Mary Cray
St. Marylebone
St. Marylebone, the Borough of
St. Mary's, Isles of Scilly
St. Mawes
St. Mawgan
St. Merryn
St. Michael's-in-the-Hamlet
St. Michael's Mount
St. Minver
St. Monan's
St. Neots (two versions)
St. Neots, 1894
St. Olaves, Norfolk Broads
St. Osyth
St. Otteridge
St. Pancras, (the Borough of –
St. Patrick   two versions)
St. Stephen
St. Teath
Salcombe
Sale (two versions)
Salford (two versions – colour variation only)
Salisbury
Salisbury, the City of
Saltaire (two versions)
Saltash
Saltburn-by-the-Sea (three versions)
Saltcoats
Saltfleet
Saltford
Saltwood
Sandbach
Sandbank, Argyllshire
Sandgate, Kent (two versions)
Sandgate, Kent, The Official Seal of
Sandhurst
Sandown, Isle of Wight (two versions)
Sandquhar
Sandringham
Sandsend (two versions)
Sandwich
Sandy
Sandy, the Manor of
Sanquhar
Sark (Sercq), Channel Isles
Saundersfoot

Saunton
Sawbridgeworth
Sawley
Saxilby
Saxmundham
Scalby
Scalby, The Manor of
Scallaway, Shetland Isles (two versions)
Scarborough (two versions)
Scarborough, the Seal of
Scilly Isles, The Ancient Arms of Star Castle, 1727
Scone
Scotland, The Royal Arms of
Scotland, the Badge of
Scotland, the Crest of
Scotswood-on-Tyne
Scotter
Scunthorpe
Scunthorpe, Seal of
Scunthorpe & Frodingham U.D.C.
Seacombe
Seacombe-cum-Poulton
Seaford I
Seaford II
Seaford, Ye ancient port of
Seaforth
Seaforth (See Waterloo)
Seamill
Seascale (two versions)
Seaton
Seaton, Devon
Seaton Carew
Seaview, Isle of Wight (four versions)
Sedbergh
Sedgefield, Co.Durham
Sedlescombe
Selby
Selkirk (two versions)
Selsey (two variations of colour)
Sennen
Sennybridge
Settle
Seven Kings
Sevenoaks, Kent (four versions)
Seven Sisters
Severn Beach
Shaftesbury
Shanklin, Isle of Wight (two versions)
Shap
Shardlow
Sharpness, The Gloucester & Berkeley Canal, 1793
Shebbear
Sheepwash
Sheerness
Sheffield

Shefford
Shenfield and Hutton
Shepherd's Bush
Shepherdswell, Dover
Shepley
Shepperton-on-Thames
Sheppey, (See Isle of)
Shepshed
Shepton Mallet
Sherborne
Sherburn-in-Elmet
Shere
Shere, the Manor of
Sherringham
Sheringham, Seal of
Shetland Isles (See Lerwick)
Shifnal
Shildon
Shiplake
Shiplake-on-Thames
Shipley, Yorks
Shipston-on-Stour
Shipton-Bellenger
Shirebrook (two versions)
Shirehampton
Shirley
Shoeburyness
Shoeburyness-on-Sea
Shoreditch
Shoreditch, the Borough of
Shoreham
Shotley Bridge
Shotts, Scotland
Shrewsbury
Shrewsbury, Battle of, 1403
Shrewton
Shrewton - "The Lock-up"
Shrivenham
Shropshire
Sidcup (three versions)
Sidley
Sidmouth
Sileby
Silloth
Silsden, Yorks
Silsoe
Silverdale
Silverdale (See Warton)
Silverhill
Sinclairtown
Sissinghurst
Sittingbourne (two versions)
Skegness
Skelmanthorpe
Skelmorlie, Scotland
Skelton-in-Cleveland
Skerries
Skepty
Skibbereen
Skinningrove, Cleveland, Yorks
Skipsea
Skipton

Skirlaugh
Skye (See Macdonald & Macleod under Nobility)
Slane
Sleaford
Sledmere
Sleights
Sligo
Slough
Slough, the Urban District Council of, 1894
Smethwick
Snaith (three versions)
Snettisham (two versions)
Snodland, Kent
Snowdon
Snowdonia
Sodor & Man (See Ecclesiastical Section)
Soham, Cambridgeshire
Solihull
Solva, Wales
Somercoates
Somerlyton, the Norfolk Broads
Somerset
Somerset, The County of
Somerset, The County Council of
Somerton
Southall
Southam
Southampton, Arms of
Southampton, Full Arms of
Southampton, 1st Crest of & 2nd Crest of
Southampton, County of
Southampton (Royal)
Southborough (three versions)
Southbourne (See Lord Malmesbury)
Southend-on-Sea
Southend-on-Sea, The County Borough of
Southerndown
Southgate
South Milford
South Minster
South Molton
South Norwood
Southport (two versions)
Southport (77966)
South Queensferry
Southsea (two versions)
Southsea (fabricated arms, sometimes incorrectly titled "Portsmouth")
South Shields (77966)
South Shields, Full Arms
South Walsham
Southwark
Southwark, the Borough of

Southwick
South Wigston
South Wingfield
South Wingfield, Wingfield Manor
Southwold, Ancient
Southwold, First Coat
Southwold, Second Coat
South Woodford
Sowerby
Sowerby, the Manor of
Sowerby Bridge (two versions)
Spalding (two versions)
Spennymoor
Spilsby (See Sir John Franklin)
Spittal-by-the-Sea
Spittal-on-Tweed
Spofforth
Stafford
Staffordshire
Staffordshire, The County of
Staincross
Staindrop
Staines
Stainland
Staithes
Stalbridge
Stalham (four versions)
Stalybridge
Stamford (two versions)
Stanford-le-Hope (two versions)
Stanhope, Co. Durham (two versions)
Stanmore
Stanningley
Stanstead Mountfitchet
Stansted, Essex
Stansted, Kent
Stantonbury
Stanton-under-Bardon
Staplecross
Stapleford
Staplehurst
Starbeck, Yorks
Starbeck, The Manor of
Staveley (three versions)
Stepney
Stepney, The Borough of
Stevenage
Stevenston
Stevenston, The Seal of, 1719
Steyning
Steyning, 1685
Stiffkey
Stirling
Stirling, Burgh of (Sterlini Opidum)
Stirling, the Ancient Arms of the Burgh of
Stirling, the County of
Stirling (?, "Honneur Aux Dignitae"

Stockbridge
Stockport
Stocksbridge (two versions)
Stockton-on-Tees
Stockton-on-Tees Rural District
Stoke-by-Nayland
Stoke Ferry
Stoke Newington
Stoke Newington, the Borough of
Stoke-on-Trent (or Stoke-upon-Trent)
Stoke-on-Trent, the County Borough of
Stokesley
Stokesley, 1675
Stone, Staffs (three versions)
Stonehaven
Stonehouse, Glos.
Stonehouse, Devon
Stonehouse, The Historical Crest of
Stoney Middleton
Stoney Stratford (two versions)
Stoney Stratford, the Manor of
Stonor
Stornoway
Storrington (See also Duke of Norfolk)
Stourbridge
Stourport
Stow
Stowmarket (two colour variations)
Stow-on-the-Wold
Strabane
Strachur, Argyllshire (three versions)
Stranraer (two versions)
Stratford-on-Avon
Stratford-on-Avon and Shakespeare
Strathaven
Strathmiglo-on-Steeple
Strathpeffer
Strathpeffer Spa (See Nobility Section - Earl of Cromartie)
Strathtay
Stratton, Cornwall
Streatham
Streatham (See Wandsworth)
Street
Street, Cobham
Stretford, Lancs.
Stretford, The Urban District Council of
Strichen
Strines
Stromness, 1817
Stromness, Orkney Isles
Strood
Stroud

Stuartfield
Studland
Sturminster Newton
Styal
Sudbury, Suffolk (two versions)
Sudeley
Suffolk
Summerbridge
Sunbury-on-Thames
Sunderland
Sunningdale
Sunningdale, Coworth Park (See Nobility - Earl of Derby)
Sunninghill (two versions)
Surbiton
Surfleet
Surrey
Surrey, The Seal of the County Council
Sussex (two varieties, colour variations)
Sutherland
Sutton, N. Riding of Yorkshire
Sutton, Surrey
Sutton Benger
Sutton Bridge, Holland, Lincs.
Sutton Coldfield
Sutton Coldfield, The Royal Town of
Sutton-in-Ashfield
Sutton-in-Craven
Sutton-on-Hull
Sutton-on-Sea
Sutton-on-Trent
Sutton Valence
Swadlincote
Swaffham
Swalwell
Swanage (two versions)
Swanland
Swanley
Swansea (two versions)
Swansea, Full Arms
Swansea - The City's Insignia
Sway
Swindon
Swindon, Wilts.
Swineshead
Swinton
Sydenham
Sydenham (See Lewisham)
Symond's Yat
Symond's Yat, Manor of
Syston

Tadcaster (three versions)
Tadworth (two versions)
Tain, Scotland (two versions)
Talgarth (two versions)
Talke
Talsarnau

Talybont, Wales
Talysarn, The Seal of
Tamworth
Tankerton
Tarbet
Tarbert, Argyllshire
Tarbert, Harris, Scotland
Tarland
Tarporley
Tarves, Scotland
Tarvin
Tattenhall
Taunton
Taunton - "Tau-and-Tun"
Taunton, The Common Seal of the Borough of
Tavistock
Tavistock, The Borough of
Tayport
Tean
Teddington
Teignmouth (two versions)
Tenby
Tenterden
Terrington St.Clements
Tetbury
Tettenhall
Tewkesbury
Tewkesbury, The Borough of
Thame
Thames Ditton, The Seal of the Surrey County Council
Thatcham
Thaxted
Thaxted, The Seal of the Mayor and Burgesses of the Borough of
Theale
Thetford
Theydon Bois
Thirsk, Manor of
Thornaby-on-Tees
Thornbury
Thornbury, Gloucestershire
Thorndon
Thorne (two versions)
Thorner
Thorngumbald
Thornham
Thornhill
Thornton Cleveleys
Thornton Dale
Thornton Heath
Thornton-le-Dale
Thornton-le-Fylde
Thorp Arch
Thorpe
Thorpe, The Manor of (two varieties)(one is Dovedale)
Thrapston (See George Washington under Nobility Section)

Three Bridges
Thrumpton
Thurles
Thurso
Thurso, Caithness. The Seal of the Burgh of
Tibshelf
Ticehurst
Tickhill
Tideswell
Tidworth (two versions)
Tighnabruaich, Scotland
Tilbury (two versions)
Tilehurst
Tillicoultry
Tilshead
Timperley
Tintagel
Tintagel, The Seal of the Mayor and Burgesses of the Borough of
Tintwistle
Tipperary
Tiptree
Tiptree, The Manor of
Tisbury
Tissington
Tiverton
Tobermory
Tobermory, The Burgh of, 1788 – 1875
Toddington
Todmorden
Tonbridge
Tong, Bradford
Tongue, Sutherlandshire
Tonypandy (two versions)
Tonyrefail
Toomebridge, Ireland
Tooting - The Seal of Surrey County Council
Topcliffe
Topsham
Torpoint
Torquay
Torrington (77966)
Totland
Totland Bay
Totley
Totnes (77966)
Tottenham (two versions)
Totton
Toward
Tow Law
Towyn
Towyn-on-Sea (three versions)
Tralee (two versions)
Tramore (three versions)
Trawsfynydd
Trearddur Bay (three versions)
Tredegar
Trefriw (two versions)
Tregaron

Tregaron, The Manor of
Trehafod
Treharris
Treherbert
Tremadoc
Trent, Sherborne, Dorset
Trentham
Treorchy (two versions)
Trevone
Trevor
Trimdon, Co.Durham (two versions)
Trimdon Colliery
Trimingham
Trimley
Tring (three versions)
Troon
Troon, The Burgh of, 1897
Troon, The Town Council of the Burgh of
Trowbridge
Truro (also without Supporters)
Tullamore
Tunbridge Wells
Tunbridge Wells, Royal
Tunbridge Wells, The Borough of
Tunbridge Wells, A souvenir of (also appears un-named)
Tunstall
Turriff, Scotland. The Burgh of (three versions)
Tuxford
Tweedmouth
Twerton
Twickenham (two versions)
Twyford, Berks. (two versions)
Twyford, Hants.
Tylorstown
Tynemouth
Tynemouth (See also North Shields)
Tysoe

Uckfield
Uckfield, The Urban District Council of
Uffington
Ulceby
Uley
Ullapool
Ullswater
Ulster
Ulverstone (two versions)
Uphill
Upminster
Upminster (See Romford)
Upnor
Upper Clatford
Upper Largo, Fife
Upper Norwood (two versions)
Upton

Upton-on-Severn
Upton-on-Severn, the Manor of
Upwell
Upwey
Upwey, the Manor of
Urmston (two versions)
Usk
Uttoxeter
Uxbridge

Valley, Wales
Ventnor
Villa Cardiff

Waddeson (four versions)
Wadebridge
Wadhurst (two versions)
Wainfleet
Wakefield
Walberswick
Wales (Red Dragon of Wales)
Wales, Arms of - "Cymru am Byth" (two varieties)
Walkhampton
Wallasey (two versions)
Wallasey, including Seacombe
Wallingford
Wallingford, The Seal of
Wallington (two versions, one being the Seal of the Surrey County Council)
Walls, Shetland
Wallsend
Walmer
Walney Island
Walsall
Walsall, The Borough of
Walsall including Bloxwich
Walsingham
Waltham Palace - founded by Henry of Blois
Walthamstow
Walton, Suffolk
Walton-le-Dale
Walton-on-Thames
Walton-on-the-Hill
Walton-on-the-Naze
Wandsworth
Wandsworth, including Putney
Wandsworth, including Streatham
Wangford
Wanlockhead, Dumfries
Wanstead (two versions)
Wantage
Warbleton
Warborough
Ware
Wareham
Wargrave
Wargrave-on-Thames
Warkworth

Llandudno

Llantrisant Town Trust 1889

Aberystwyth (Ancient)

Aberystwyth depicted on a Welsh Hat.

Aberdare

Borth

Welshpool

Bettws-y-Coed

Llanberis shown here on a Bust of The Prince of Wales.

Llanberis

Arms of Wales   A later version than the other two Welsh Arms.

Wales
Three Varieties of the same Arms.

Cymru Am Byth

Warminster
Warrenpoint
Warrington
Warslow
Warsop
Warton, the Manor of -
Silverdale, Lancs.
Warwick
Warwick, The Seal of (two versions)
Warwickshire
Washington, Sussex
Watchet
Waterford
Waterford, the City of
Waterloo
Waterloo, with Seaforth, Lancs.
Waterlooville
Watford (two versions)
Wath-upon-Dearne (two versions one Wath-on-Dearne)
Watlington, 1685 (two versions)
Watton, Norfolk
Waverton
Wealdstone, Middx.
Wedmore
Wednesbury
Wednesbury, The Borough of
Weedon
Weedon, The Manor of
Weedon Beck
Week St.Mary
Welford
Welford-on-Avon
Welland, The Corporation of
Well Hall
Wellingborough
Wellington
Wellington, Salop
Wellington, Somerset
Wells, Somerset. The City of
Wells-next-the-Sea
Welshpool
Welton
Welwyn (two versions)
Wem (two versions)
Wembley
Wembley, The Urban District Council of
Wembley, The Seal of the Urban District Council of
Wemyss
Wendover (two versions)
West Auckland
West Ayton
Westbourne
West Bromwich
West Bromwich, The Borough of
West Burton
Westbury

Westbury-on-Severn
Westbury-on-Trym
West Butterwick
Westcliffe-on-Sea (three versions)
West Dereham
Westerham (two versions)
Westgate-on-Sea, Kent
West Ham
West Ham, The Borough of (three versions)
West Hartlepool
West Hoathly
West Houghton
West Kilbride (two versions)
West Kirby
West Kirby, The Seal of, 1st. Ed. 1901
West Kirby & Hoylake (77966)
West Lavington
West Linton
West Looe
West Lulworth
West Malling, Kent
Westminster, The City of (two varieties)
Westmorland (two versions)
West Norwood - In the Metropolitan Borough of Lambeth, 1900
Westonbirt
Weston-super-Mare (two versions)
Westport
Westray, Orkney
West Riding of Yorkshire
West Stanley
West Sussex
West Sussex County Council
West Tarring
Westward Ho
West Worthing
Wetherby
Wexford (two versions)
Weybridge (two versions)
Weybourne (See Earl of Orford)
Weymouth, The Seal of
Weymouth and Melcombe Regis
Weymouth and Melcombe Regis, The Seal of
Whaley Bridge
Whalley
Whaplode
Whatstandwell (two versions)
Wheathampstead (two versions)
Whilish
Whitburn
Whitby
Whitchurch, Hants.
Whitchurch, Salop.
Whitehaven (two versions)
Whitehead (three versions)
Whitfield
Whithorn, The Corporate Seal of

Whiting Bay, Scotland
Whitland, Pembrokeshire
Whitley Bay
Whitstone
Whittington
Whittington Moor
Whittlesea
Whitwell, Herts.
Whitwick
Whorlton-in-Swainby, Cleveland
Whyteleafe
Wibsey
Wick
Wick, The Seal of the Burgh, 1589 (three versions)
Wickford (two versions)
Wickham
Wickham Market (two versions)
Wicklow
Wickwar
Widnes
Wigan
Wigston
Wigston Magna
Wigton
Wigtown
Willenhall
Willesden
Willesden Green
Willington Quay-on-Tyne
Williton
Willoughby
Wilmslow
Wilsden
Wilton
Wiltshire
Wimbledon
Wimborne
Wimborne, The Seal of
Wincanton
Winchburgh
Winchcombe, 1558
Winchelsea
Winchester, The City of
Winchester, Seal of
Winchester
Windermere
Windhill
Windlesham
(Windleshaw) Arms on Chantry -
"En Dieu Est Mon Esperance" (See Sir Thomas Gerard, Section AC6)
Windsor
Winfield, The Manor of
Wingate
Winscombe
Winsford
Winslow
Winslow, Manor of
Winterton (two versions)
Wirksworth

Wisbech, Crest of the Borough of Wisbech
Wisbech, The Borough of
Wisbech, The Seal of
Wishart
Wishaw
Wistow
Witham
Withernsea (two versions)
Withernwick
Withyham
Witley Camp
Witney
Wiveliscombe, 1775 (two versions)
Woburn Sands, Bucks (three versions)
Woking (two versions)
Wokingham
Wolsingham
Wolsley Bridge
Wolstanton
Wolston
Wolverhampton
Wolverley
Wolverton (three versions)
Wombwell (three versions)
Wooburn
Wooburn Green
Woodbridge (two versions)
Woodford (See Earl Cowley)
Woodford Halse
Wood Green
Wood Green U.D.C.
Woodhall Spa
Woodhouse, Ireland
Woodhouse, Yorks.
Woodhouse Eaves
Woodstock
Woodville
Wool
Woolacombe (three versions)
Woolhampton
Woolsery
Woolston
Woolwich (two versions)
Woore and Pipe Gate
Wootton, Isle of Wight
Wootton Bassett
Worcester
Worcester, The City of (two versions)
Worcestershire
Workington
Worksop (two versions)
Worle
Worplesdon
Worthing - Early Arms, (Argent field)
Worthing, (Azure field)
Wotton-under-Edge
Wrexham
Writtle

	2. AFRICA and ADJACENT ISLES	3. ASIA	4. AUSTRALASIA and PACIFIC
Wrotham	Abyssinia	Bethel	Adelaide
Wroxall, Isle of Wight	Alexandria	Bombay	Adelaide, City of
Wroxham	Bloemfontein	Burmah	Auckland, N.Z., The City of
Wybunbury	Bulawayo	Calcutta	Australia
Wycombe	Cairo	Ceylon (two versions)	Australia, Arms of
Wye	Cape of Good Hope (two versions)	China	Australia, Commonwealth of
Wyke	Cape Town	Colombo	Brisbane
Wylam-on-Tyne (two versions)	Dundee	Hong Kong	Cairns
Wylde Green, The Royal Town of	Durban	India	Christchurch, N.Z.
Wymondham	East London	Jerusalem	Dunedin
	Egypt (two versions)	Joppa	Dunedin, City of. Incorporated 1865
Yarm-on-Tees (three versions)	Elizabethville	Kuala Lumpur	Dunedin, Municipality of, 1865
Yarmouth, Isle of Wight	Funchal, Madeira	Madras	Fiji
Yarmouth, Isle of Wight, The Seal of	Grahamstown	Malacca	Freemantle, W.A.
Yatton, Somerset	Harrismith, O.R.C.	Malay Straits, The	Geelong, Australia (A Souvenir from the City of)
Yeadon	Johannesburg (two varieties)	Mandalay	Gisborne
Yeaveley	Kimberley	Penang	Hobart
Yelverton	Kroonstad	Russia, The Arms of Imperial	Ipswich
Yeovil (two versions)	Ladysmith, Natal, The Borough of	Russia	Japan
Ynyscynhaiarn (See Portmadoc)	Las Palmas, Grand Canary	Shanghai	Launceston (Tasmania)
Ynyshir	Lourenço Marques	Singapore	Levuka, Municipality of, Ovalau, Fiji
York, The City of	Madeira	Straits Settlements	Melbourne
York, The City Arms and Regalia	Mauritius		Melbourne, City of
Yorkshire	Morocco		Napier
Youghal	Mossel Bay		New Plymouth
Yoxford	Muizenborg-Kalk Bay		New South Wales
Ystradgynlais	Natal		New Zealand 'Kia-ora'
Ystrad Mynach	Orange River Colony		New Zealand (two versions)
	Oudtshoorn		New Zealand, Dominion of
	Pietermaritzberg		New Zealand, Dominion of ("From Christchurch")
	Pietermaritzberg, The City of		North Auckland
	Port Alfred		Perth (W.Australia)
	Port Elizabeth		Perth, The City of (two versions)
	Port Said		Queensland
	Potchefstroom		Queensland, Badge of
	Pretoria		Rockhampton
	Province of the Cape of Good Hope		Rockhampton, The City of
	Rhodesia		South Australia
	St.Helena		South Australia, State Badge of
	Sakkara		Southport
	Salisbury, Rhodesia		Sydney
	Santa Cruz de Teneriffe		Sydney, City of
	Simonstown (Cape of Good Hope)		Tasmania
	Teneriffe		Tonga
	Transvaal, The Province of		Toowcob.
	Tunis		Toowoomba
	Uitenhage, The Municipality of United South Africa		Victoria
	Vryheid		Wanganui
	Walmer		Wellington, N.Z.
	Wynberg		Wellington, 1842
	Z.A.R. (Zuid Afrika Republic)		Western Australia

Albert
Alençon
Amiens
Amsterdam
Antwerpen
Antwerpen Province
Anvers
Arcachon
Arles
Arnhem
Arras
Avignon
Baden-Baden
Bad Nauheim
Bagneres-de-Bigorre
Bapaume
Barcelona
Barum, Norway
Basel (or Basle)
Bayeux
Bayonne
Bayreuth
Beauvais
Belfort, Belgium
Belgium (two versions)
Bergen
Bergerac
Berlin
Bern (or Berne)
Besançon-les-Bains
Biarritz
Bilbao
Blankenberghe (two versions)
Bonn
Bordeaux
Boulogne
Boulogne-sur-Mer
Bourges
Breda (Holland)
Bremen
Brest
Bretagne
Brittany
Brugge (or Bruges)
Brussels (or Bruxelles)
Cadiz
Calais (two versions, one marked 1347-1558)
Cambrai
Cannes (two versions)
Chantilly (two versions)
Chantilly (Armes de Condé)
Charlottenburg
Chatelard
Chatelard, Montreux
Cherbourg
Cherbourg, Ville de
Christiana, Norway
Coblenz
Coln-a-Rh (or Cologne)
Como, Italy

Compiegne
Constanz Bodensee, Germany
Cordoba, Spain
Coutainville, France
Coutances, France
Cyprus
Danzig
Daves Platz, Switzerland
Denmark
Denmark, Royal Arms of
Dieppe
Dignes
Dinant
Doullens, France
Dresden
Dunkerque (or Dunkirk)
Dusseldorf
Engelberg
Essen
Euzkadi
Evian-les-Bains
El Ferrol, Spain
Firenze (or Florence)
Flushing
Fontainebleau
France (Republique Français)
Frankfurt
Freiberg
Freiberg-im-Breisgau
Gand (or Ghent)
Geneva
Germany
Ghent (or Gand)
Gibraltar
Granada
Greece
Grenoble
Grindelwald
Grisons
Hague, The
Hamburg
Hanover
Hardelot-Plage
Hasselt, Ville de
Heidelburgh
Heyst s-Mer
Holland
Honfleur (two versions)
Innsbruck
Interlaken (two versions)
Italia (or Italy)
Jent
Karlsruhe-im-Baden
Kissingen
Klosters, (Ct.Graubünden) Switzerland
Københaven
Lausanne (two versions)
Le Havre
Leipzig
Leon, Spain
Limoges
Lisboa, Mui Nombreleal Cidade da

Lisboa
Lourdes (Souvenir de)
Lucerne (or Luzern)
Luchon
Lugano
Lyons
Madrid
Mainz
Malaga
Malta (three versions)
Marienbad
Marken
Melun, France
Middelberg
Milano (or Milan)
Molde, Norway
Monnikendam
Monte Carlo
Montreux
Montreux - Chatelard
Montreux - Les Planches
Montreux - Veytaux
Montreux - Chatelard, les Planches, Veytaux
München
Munster
Namur
Nancy
Naples
Neuchatel
Nieupoort
Niort, France
Nivelles
Norge (or Norway)
Normandie
Nürnberg
Ober Ammergau
Ostende (two versions)
Palermo
Palma
Paris
Paris, Souvenir de
Pau
Peronne
Plauen-im-V.
Portugal
Le Puy
Ravenna
Reims, Ville de
Rennes
Republique Française (See also "Great Britian")
La Rochelle
La Roche-sur-Yon (two versions)
Roman States, The Arms of the
Roma (Rome)
Ronda
Rotterdam
Roubaix
Rouen
Rouen, Ville de

Roumania (or Rumania)
Russia (See Asia)
St. Lo
St. Malo
St. Moritz Bad
St. Quentin
San Sebastian
Salzburg
San Remo
Schaffhausen
Schweiz
Schwyz
Senf
Servia, Kingdom of
Sevilla
S. Gravenhage
Sicilia, Emblema Della
Sluis
Soissons
Spa, Belgium
Spain (or Espana)
Stavelot
Stettin
Stockholm
Stockholm Stads Vapen
Strasbourg
Stuttgart
Sweden
Switzerland
Tirol, The (Tyrol)
Toledo
Torino (Turin)
Toulon-sur-mer
Toulouse
Trento
Trieste
Tromso
Trondhjem
Trouville
Unterwalden
Uri
Valencia
Valletta, Malta
Versailles, Armes de
Versailles
Venice
Vevey
Vigo, The City of
Vlaanderen
Vlissingen
Volendam
Waadt
Waterloo, Belgium
Wavre
Westende
Westvlaanderen
Wien
Wiesbaden
Ypres
Zaandam
Zeeland
Zoppot
Zug
Zurich

München

Hamburg

Basel

Grindelwald

Amiens

Brugge

Marienbad

Montreaux. Chatelard, les
Planches, Veytaux.

Torino (Turin)

Euzkadi

Arms of Great Britian and Republique Française linked

Monte Carlo

Sluis

39

6. THE AMERICAS and ADJACENT ISLES

Antofagasta, Chile
Argentina
Bahamas
Banff, Canada
Barbados (or Barbadoes) (colour variation)
Belleville, Canada
Bermuda (three versions)
Boston, U.S.A.
Brazil
British Columbia
British Honduras
Buenos Aires
Calgary
Canada (two versions)
Canada, (Arms of) the Dominion of, Sometimes a place name is added, e.g.
Canada – Tidworth
Champlain, Canada – 1608
Chicago
Chile
Chile (Recuerdo de Chile)
Chilliwach (B.C.) Canada
Chilliwach (Souvenir of)
Cornwall, Ontario
Denton, North Carolina, 1857; Haughton, 1877
Edmonton, Canada
Falkland Islands, The Ancient Arms of
Falkland Islands, The Modern Arms of (time of Edward VII)
Falkland Islands, The Modern Arms of (time of George V)
Fernie, Canada
Florida
Fort William, Canada
Fredericton, New Brunswick
Grand Falls, Canada
Guelph, Ontario
Halifax, Canada
Halifax, Nova Scotia
Hamilton, Bermuda
Jamaica
Kaslo, Canada
Kelowna, Canada
Kingston, Jamaica
Kingston, Ontario, The City of
Laggan, Canada
Manitoba
Melita, Canada
Moncton, New Brunswick
Montreal
Nassau
Nelson, Canada
New Westminster, Canada, The City of
New York
New York, State of
Nicaragua

Nova Scotia
Ontario
Ottawa
Panama
Port Arthur
Port Stanley
Quebec
Quebec, The City of (two versions)
Rat Portage
Red Deer, The Town of
Rossland
St. John, New Brunswick
San Paulo
Toronto (two versions)
Trenton, Ontario
United States of America (E Pluribus Unum')
Valparaiso
Vancouver, B.C., The City of
Venezuela
Vernon, Canada
Victoria, B.C., The City of (two versions)
Winnipeg, Canada, The City of (three versions)
Winnipeg, Canada (The Arms of King Edward VII)
Yorktown, Virginia

Tasmania

Hobart (Tasmania)

A Large Trinket Tray bearing eight Commonwealth and Empire Arms; it can be dated by the Arms of King George V in the centre.

Commonwealth of Australia

State Badge of South Australia

Durban

Cape of Good Hope

Falkland Islands

Halifax, Canada

Egypt

Cairo

Morocco

Santa Crux de Tenerife

41

B. Royal

1. BRITISH: a) KINGS

Royal arms were a speciality of Ritchie & Co., Station China Stall, Stoke-on-Trent, who stocked a vast range including many of the Ancient Kings of Britain. These earlier Kings would be worth + £8.00 and the later Royal Arms + £3.00–£5.00.

Alfred (two versions – one stating "born at Wantage AD 871-901", the other "A.D. 871-901".
Arthur (Arms)
Arthur (Shield) (two versions – one stating "buried at Glastonbury Abbey")
Athelstan
Brute
Cadwallader
Caractacus
Charles I
Charles II
Cymbelin
David, King of Scotland.(David Dei Gratia Rex Scottorum)
Edward the Confessor
Edward the Elder, founder of Romsey Abbey, 907
Edward the Martyr, assassinated at Corfe Castle, A.D.978
Edward I (Seat: Waltham Cross)
Edward IV (two versions)
Edward VI
Edward VII
Edward VIII
George III
George V
Harold
Henry Duke of Warwick, King of the Isle of Wight, born 1424, died 1445.
Henry I
Henry II
Henry III
Henry IV
Henry of Monmouth (Henry V)
James Stuart
Lud
Vortigern
William The Conqueror
William Rufus
(King) William Rufus
William of Orange
William III (of Orange)
Also: –
The Royal Arms of England
The Royal Arms of Scotland
Arms of the Ancient Kings of Scotland
Arms of the Ancient Kings of Cornwall

b) QUEENS

Alexandra
Alexandra (Paternal Arms of)
Anne
Anne Boleyn
Eleanor of Castile (Seat: Waltham Cross)
Elizabeth
Elizabeth ("Dieu et Mon Droit")
Her Majesty The Queen (Victoria)
Margaret of Anjou
Mary
Mary, Queen of Scots
Victoria
H.M. Queen Victoria

c) PRINCES and PRINCESSES

Princess Alice, Arms of the Beloved
Princess Anne, Arms of the Beloved
Black Prince (Arms of)
Black Prince (War Shield)
Black Prince (Peace Shield)
Prince Charlie Stewart, (Arms used by)
Prince Charles Stewart
Edward of Carnarvon
Edward of Carnarvon, Prince of Wales
Owen Glendower
Owen Glendwr
Prince Edward (Longshanks), Conqueror of the Battle of Evesham, 1265
Prince of Wales (later Edward VII)
Prince of Wales (later George V)
Prince of Wales (the Badge of)
H.R.H. The Prince of Wales
H.R.H. The Prince of Wales, K.G., Baron Killarney
The Princess of Wales (the Paternal Arms of)
H.R.H. Princess Royal (the Crest of)
Prince Llewellyn
Prince Gryffith ap Cynan Founder of 1st Royal Tribe of Wales
Prince Rhys ap Tewdwr Mawr – Founder of 2nd Royal Tribe of Wales
Prince Blethyn ap Cynfyn – Founder of 3rd Royal Tribe of Wales
Prince Ethelystan Glodrydd – Founder of 4th Royal Tribe of Wales
Prince Jestyn ap Gwrgant – Founder of 5th Royal Tribe of Wales
H.R.H. Princess Mary (also found linked with Viscount Lascelles)
Prince Owen of Gwynedd – Badge of the Prince of North Wales, and Lord of Snowdon. (Seat: Abersoch)
Prince Owen of Gwynedd - Abersoch, Badge of
Prince Owen Glendower
Prince Wynn of Gwydyr, 1597
Wynn of Gwydr

2. OTHERS

Alphonso XIII of Spain
Coel
Hamlet, Prince of Denmark (two sizes)
Henry of Blois
Henry of Navarre, King of France
Napoleon I
Stanley, King of Man

N.B. See also C. NOBILITY & PERSONAL

Edward The Confessor

Arms of King George III

First Royal Tribe of Wales

Second Royal Tribe of Wales

Arms of H.M. King George V

Arms of H.M. Queen Mary

Third Royal Tribe of Wales

Fourth Royal Tribe of Wales

Arms of Queen Victoria

Arms of King Edward VII

Fifth Royal Tribe of Wales

Prince Llewelyn

King William Rufus

Ancient Kings of Cornwall

Henry of Monmouth. (Named on base)

Arms of Edward of Carnarvon Prince of Wales (Named on base)

43

The majority of the arms in this section are scarce, being of interest mainly in the locality in which they were stocked. Therefore, the number sold would be somewhat less than the town arms of a particular area.

The majority of Nobility and Personal Arms are worth + £3.00 − + £8.00

1. DUKES

Duke of Argyll (Seats: Clynder, Inverary Castle, Kirn, Roseneath, Tighnabruaich)
Duke of Argyll (Iona)
Duke of Athlone
Duke of Athole (Seat: Killiecrankie)
Duke of Beaufort, Lord of the Manor of Brynmawr
Duke of Bedford, Lord Lieutenant of Middlesex. (Seats: Woburn, Woburn Sands)
Duke of Buccleugh (Seats: Boughton House, Near Kettering & Geddington)
Second Duke of Buckingham — died at Kirby Moor Side, 1687
Duke of Castle Golspie
Duke of Chandos (Seat: Edgware)
Duke of Devonshire
Duke of Edinburgh
Duke of Fife, Lord Lieutenant of London (Seat: Dufftown)
Duke of Gordon (Seat: Newtonmore)
Duke of Hamilton (Seats: Brodick, Corrie, Larnach)
Duke of Lancaster
Duke of Manchester (Seat: Kimbolton Castle)
Duke of Marlborough
Duke of Montrose (Seats: Aberfoyle, also at Brodick, Lamlash, Whiting Bay)
Duke of Newcastle-under-Lyme
Duke of Norfolk
Duke of Norfolk, Lord of the Manor of Storrington
Duke of Northumberland (Seats: Manor of Whitley Bay and Twickenham)
Duke of Portland (Seats: Ashington, Whitwell & Hirst)
Duke of Richmond
Duke of Richmond and Gordon (Seats: Fochabers & Fort Gordon)
Duke of Roxburgh
Duke of Rutland
Duke of Sutherland (Seat: Dunrobin Castle, Golspie)
Duke of Wellington
Duke of Westminster
Duke of York

2. MARQUISES

Marquis of Abergavenny, K.G.
Marquis of Anglesey
Marquis of Bath (Arms)
Marquis of Bath (Crest)
Marquis of Breadalbane (Seat: Aberfeldy and Kenmore)
Marquis of Bute
Marquis of Conyngham
Marquis of Downshire (Seat: Newcastle, Co.Down)
Marquis of Exeter
Marquis of Huntly (Seat: Aboyne)
Marquis of Lansdowne
Marquis of Londonderry
Marquis of Normanby
Marquis of Salisbury (Seat: Hatfield)
Marquis of Zetland

3. EARLS and COUNTESSES

Earl of Aberdeen
Earl of Airlie
Earl of Ancaster (Seats: Callander, Grimsthorpe)
Earl of Annesley
Earl of Antrim (Seats: Glenariffe, Cushendall and Glenarm Castle)
Earl of Antrim, 'Giants Causeway'
Earl of Beaconsfield
Earl Brownlow
Earl of Caithness
Earl of Caithness (Seat: John O'Groats)
Earl of Carlisle (Seat: Brampton)
Earl Carrington (Seat: Gwydr Castle)
Earl of Carnarvon
Earl of Carnarvon, Lord High Steward of Newbury
Earl of Cawdor
First Earl of Chester — Hugh Lupus
Earl of Chiddingfold (Seat: Shillinglee Park, Chiddingfold)
Earl Cowley — Lord of the Manor of Woodford
Earl of Crawford, Kilbirnie
Earl of Cromartie (Seat: Strathpeffer Spa)
Earl of Dalhousie (Seat: Brechin Castle)
Earl of Dartmouth
Earl of Derby (Seat: Coworth Park, Sunningdale)
Earl of Derwentwater
The Last Earl of Derwentwater — James Ratcliffe — Executed in 1716.
Earl of Devon
Earls of Douglas
Earl of Dunraven (Seat: Dunraven Castle, Southerndown)
Earl of Durham
Earl Egerton (Seat: Chorlton-cum-Hardy, Tatton)
Earl of Erroll
Earl of Feversham (Seat: Duncombe Park, Helmsley)
Earl Fitzwilliam
Earl of Galloway. (Seat: Cumloden, Newton Stewart)
Earl of Glasgow
Earl of Gosford (Acheson)
Earl of Haddington (Seat: Earlston)
Earl of Iddesleigh
Earl of Ilchester (Seat: Abbotsbury Castle)
Earl of Leicester (Seat: Holkham Hall, Norfolk)

Rudyerd of Rudyard Obverse

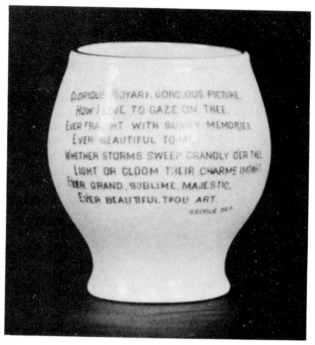

Reverse showing Verse by George Heath

C.W.D. Perrins, Ardross Castle, Alness.

Marsham Townshend, Frognall, Sidcup

Sir Thomas Lucy of Charlecote

Shakespeares Arms (on Shakespeares Font)

Arms of Dorothy Vernon Impaled with Arms of her Husband, Sir John Manners.

Crest of John Keble

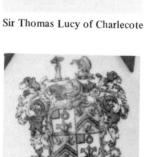

F. Algernon Dorrien-Smith, Esq. Lord Proprietor of the Isles of Scilly.

Admiral Lord Nelson

Earl of Lindsay (Seat: Kilconquhar)
Earl of Lonsdale
Earl of Malmesbury
Earl Manvers
Earl of Mar and Kellie
Earl of Masefield (Seat: Scone Palace, Perth)
Earl of Moray
Earl of Morton (Seat: Aberdour Castle) (two versions)
Earl of Mount-Edgcumbe (Seat: The Manor of Bere Alston)
Earl of Orford, Lord of the Manor of Weybourne (Norfolk)
Earl of Pembroke
Earl of Pomfret (Seat: Towcester) (two versions)
Earl of Radnor
Earl of Rosebery (Seat: Cheddington)
Earl of St.Germans
Ela, Countess of Salisbury, Founder of Lacock Abbey
Earl of Scarborough
Earl of Seafield (Seat: Cullen) "Stand Fast"
Earl of Seaford
Earl of Shrewsbury and Talbot (Seat: Alton Towers)
Earl of Southesk
Earl Spencer, Lord of the Manor of Barnes
Earl of Stair (Seat: Castle Kennedy)
Earl of Stanhope, Lord of the Manor of Holsworthy
Earl of Stanmore
Earl Patrick Stewart, The Lord of Zetland, and builder of Scalloway Castle
Earl of Strathmore (Seat: Rowlands Gill)
Earls of Surrey. Arms of the Lords of the Manor of Thorne 1066-1347
Earl of Tankerville (Seats: Wooler, Chillingham Castle)
Earl of Tatton
Guy, Earl of Warwick
Earl of Westmorland
First Earl of Westmorland, Ralph Nevill, Lord of the Manor of Kettlewell.
Earl of Winchelsea and Nottingham (Seat: Weldon)
Earl of Winterton (Seat: Shillinglee Park, Chiddingfold)
Earl of Zetland

Viscount Downe 'Driffield'
Viscount Lambton (Seat: Chester-le-Street)
Viscount Lascelles (also found linked with H.R.H. Princess Mary)
Viscount Tredegar (Seat: Ruperra Castle, Nr.Machin)

Lord Ampthill of Ampthill
Lord Annesley (Seat Castlewellan, Newcastle, Co.Down)
Lord Annesley of Zetland
Lord Armstrong (Seats: Jesmond Dene, Craigside, Rothbury)
Lord Ashburnham
Lord Ashburton
Lord Barnard (Seat: Raby Castle)
Lord Basing
Lord Beaconsfield
Lord Braybrooke (Seat: Bracknell)
Lady Eleanor Butler, with the Hon. Sarah Ponsonby, one of the original ladies of Llangollen
Lord Byron
Lord Camoys (Seat: Stonor Park)
Lord Chesham
Lord Clinton, Lord of the Manor of Beer (Seat: Beer)
Lord Crewe (the late) Bishop of Durham
Lord Cross
Lord De L'Isle (Seat: Penshurst)
Lord De Ramsey
Lord Denman (Seat: Stoney Middleton)
Lord Ellenborough (Seat: Windlesham Court)
Lord Falmouth, Lord of the Manor of Mullion
Lady Godiva
Lord Glanusk, Lord of the Manor of Llangasmarch Wells
Lord Harlech
Lord Hothfield
Lord Howard of Glossop
Lord Kitchener
Lord Leconfield
Lord Londesborough, Baron (Seats: Tadcaster, Market Weighton)
Lord Londonderry (Seats: Carnlough, Seaham Harbour)
Lord Lovat (Seat: Beaufort Castle, Beauly, Invernesshire)
Lord Lucan (Seat: Laleham House, Staines)
Lord Macdonald (Portree)
Lord Malmesbury, Lord of the Manor of Southbourne
Lord Malmesbury
Lord Melbourne
Lord Muncaster
Lord Nelson (Admiral)
Lord Nelson (Seat: San Josef)
Lord Newborough (Seat: Bryn Llewellyn, Festiniog)

Lord Panmure (the late) (Seat: Brechin Castle)
Lord Penrhyn, Lord of the Manor of Aber
Lord Portsmouth (Seat: Hurstbourne Park, Whitchurch,Hants.)
Lord Raglan
Lord Randolph Churchill
Lord Ravensworth (Seat: Low Fell, Co.Down)
Lord Rolle-Douglas
Lord Rothschild (Seat: Tring Park, Tring)
Lord Sackville
Lord Savile
Lord St.Audries, Lord of the Manor of St.Otteridge
Lord St.Levan (Seat: St.Michael's Mount)
Lords of Thorne
Lord Tredegar (Seat: Ruperra Castle, Nr. Machin)

Duke of Northumberland

Earl of Cromartie, Strathpeffer Spa.

Lord Lovat 'Beauly'

Lord Malmesbury, Lord of the Manor of Southbourne

Early Arms were named on the base only, as shown here.

Arms of Duke of Devonshire. Shown here on early Jug.

Earl of Seafield

Earl of Beaconsfield

Marquis of Salisbury 'Hatfield'

Viscount Tredegar. Seat: Ruperra Castle, Nr. Machen.

Earl of Radnor

Arms of Sir Walter Scott

Sir William Wallace

6. BARONETS and KNIGHTS

Sir E. Antrobus, Bt. (Seat: Amesbury Abbey)
Sir R.B.M. Blois, Bt. Lord of the Manors of Blythburgh and Yoxford
Sir Robert Burnett of Leys, Bt. (Seat: Banchory)
Sir J. Colquhoun, Bt. (Seat: Arrocharhouse, North Britain)
Sir George Colthurst, Bt. (Seat: Blarney Castle)
Sir Francis Drake
Sir Francis Drake (Crest of)
Sir Edmund Elton (Seat: Clevedon Court)
Sir John Franklin (from a brass in Parish Church, Spilsby)
Sir Thomas Gerard of Bryn (Manor of Charlton)
Sir Thomas Gerard of Kingsley & Bryn. (Arms on Windleshaw Chantry.)
Sir Humphrey Gilbert
Sir John Gilmour, Bt. (Seat: Lundin Links)
Sir Thomas Hesketh, Bt. (Seats: Easton Neston, Towcester)
Sir Thomas Lucy (Seat: Charlecote)
Sir John Manners/Dorothy Vernon (Joint Arms)
Sir S. Maryon-Wilson, Bt. Lord of the Manor of Charlton
Sir John Moore (Founder of Shorncliffe Camp, Hythe)
Sir Hugh Myddleton (Seat: Winchmore Hill)
Rev. Sir F.A.G. Ouseley, Bt. (St. Michael's College, Tenbury)
Sir Goddard Pemberton
Sir W. Phillimore, Bt. (Seat: The Coppice, Shiplake)
Sir Alan de Plunkenet (From Corfe Castle)
Sir F.A.De La Pole, Bt., Lord of The Manor of Colyton
Sir Walter Raleigh
Sir Titus Salt, Bt., Founder of Saltaire
Sir Walter Scott
Sir Walter Strickland, Bt. Lord of the Manor of Robin Hood's Bay
Sir Ian Stuart
Sir William Wallace
Sir Symone de Warde, 1270 (Seat: Guiseley)

7. POETS and WRITERS

Acland
Burns (Note – Arms for, not of)
Lord Byron
Thomas Carlyle (Seat: Ecclefechan)
Geoffrey Chaucer
Coleridge
Courtenay
Cowper
Gilbert
Thomas Hardy
George Herbert
John Milton (Finished Paradise Lost' at Chalfont St. Giles)
John Ruskin
Sir Walter Scott
William Shakespeare (two versions
Shelley
Southey
Swinburne (See also Section A.C.8.)
Alfred Lord Tennyson
William Wordsworth

8. PERSONAL and OTHER NOBILITY

Anstruther (Seat: Kilrenny and Callordyke)
Bagot of Leven
Baildon of Baildon (Seat: Baildon, Yorks)
Baldwin of Dalton-in-Furness
Barnes, Lord of the Manor of
Bernard Balliol – Founder of Barnard Castle, 1112 A.D.
Bally Menagh of The Seven Towers (Seat: Ballymena)
Baron of Audley
The Barons of Hungerford
Barton, The Mayor of
Bildeston (Seat: Gosford)
Admiral Blake, Born at Bridgwater 1598
Botreaux
Bourne, The Baron of
De Breos of Haycastle
Walter de Bolbec, founded Blanchland Abbey 1165
Breadalbane
Brisbane of Brisbane
Brockman family of Beachborough, Arms of
Bruce (Seat: Langside)
General Buller
The Buller Family
De Burgh (Seats: West Drayton and Yiewsley)
Burnetts of Leys Barts
Butter of Faskally (Seat: Pitlochry)
Cadwgan, Lord of Mannau
Campbell of Dunstaffnage (Seat: Connel, Argyllshire)
Mrs. Campbell of Dunstaffnage (Seat: Inverawe, Taynuilt)
Campbell of Stonefield (Tarbert)
Carlin Row (Seat: Cleveland, Yorks)
Rt. Hon. J. Chamberlain
Clavering of Axwell
J.T. Clifton, Esq. (Ansdell)
(Cluny) Macpherson of Cluny (Seat: Newtonmere)
Oliver Cromwell
Darroch of Gourock
The Deedes Family of Saltwood Castle
Denton 1857 Haughton 1877 Persevere ? (See also Section (A) A.6.)
Dormer, Lord of the Manor of Flamborough
F. Algernon Dorrien-Smith, Lord Proprietor of the Isles of Scilly
Disraeli
Douglas of Tilquhille (Seat: Banchory)
Dragonis de Beurere 1070 (Seat: Hornsea)
The Dysart Arms (Seat: Buckminster)

T. Dyson, Esq. Mayor of Windsor, 1890-1891
Egremont
John of Eltham
Willoughby de Eresby (Seat: Spilsby)
The Evans Family
Farquharson of Invercauld (Seat: Ballater)
Farquharson of Invercauld (Seat: Braemar)
Farquharson of Haughton (Seat: Alford)
Ferguson (Seat: Old Deer)
Nicholas Ferrar
Robert Fitz Ranulph – Founder of Beauchief Abbey, 1183
Fitz William Family – Arms in Mablethorpe Church
Flamborough, Lords of the Manor of. Also: Former Lord of the Manor of
Forbes Arms (Seat: Alford)
Frodsham of Frodsham
Dr.Robertson Fullerton (Seat: Kilmichael, Arran)
Garvach Arms (Seat: Dallas, Scotland)
Grant of that Ilk (Freuchie and Glenmorris)
Gwydyr (See also (A) B. Royalty 1)
John of Gaunt (Seat: Reeth) (two versions)
W.E. Gladstone (Seat: Hawarden)
Glynne of Hawarden
W.H. Goss
John de Grandisson, Founder of Ottery St.Mary Church
John Greenaway of Tiverton, 1517
The Gresham Arms (Seat: Limpsfield)
The Grosvenor Arms
The Gwydr Arms
John Halle of Halle (Arms of)
John Halle of Halle, Merchant's Mark of
Hamilton of Dalzell
John Hampden
James Hargrave Harrison, Esq., Lord of the Manor of Burgh Castle
Haughton (See Denton)
Henry of Blois, Founder of Waltham Palace
Henry of Monmouth (See also B.1.)
Herbert of Llanarth
Hereward the Wake (Seat: Bourne)
Harry Hotspur, killed at the Battle of Shrewsbrury 1403
Holt of Aston Hall
Innes of Learney (Seat: Torphins)
Irvine of Drum (Seat: Drumoak)
Jack of Newbury (Arms of)
Jack of Newbury (Mark of)

Jack of Newbury (Monogram of)
John Keble (Crest of)
Keigwin of Mousehole
Kettlewell, Lord of the Manor of Kinmundy (Seat: Mintlaw)
John Kyrle (See Man of Ross)
Lea Burst (or Burat) (Seat: Holloway)
Le Strange of Hunstanton (Seat: Ringstead)
Lambeth (Seat: Hythe 1900; Norwood)
Learney Arms (Seat: Torphins)
Lord W.D.Latimer, 1327 (Seat: Danby)
Lord of the Manor of Budleigh Salterton
MacDonald
MacDonald of MacDonald, the Lord of Skye
MacDonald of Glencoe
MacGregor of Dungarvan Castle
MacKenzie of Glen Muick
MacKinnon of Strath (Seat: Broadford, Skye)
MacLeod of MacLeod (Seat: Dunvegan, Skye)
MacLeod of that Ilk (Seat: Dunvegan Castle, Skye)
MacPherson of Cluny
Man of Ross (John Kyrle) (Ross, Herefordshire)
Man of Ross, The Loyal Mark of
Margaret of Anjou
Marple Bridge, Lord of the Manor of
Marsham Townsend, Frognall, Sidcup
Menzies of Menzies (Seat: Aberfeldy)
William de Meschines, Builder of Cockermouth Castle
The Molesworth Family (Seat: Wadebridge)
Simon de Montfort — Killed at the Battle of Evesham 1265 A.D.
B.S.G. Nelthorpe, 1669
Netherby (Seat: Longtown)
Nisbet of Dirleton
The Norton Family (Seat: Malton)
Oakley Arms
William Penn
Penns of Stoke Park, Slough
C.W.D. Perrins, Esq. (Seat: Ardross Castle, Alness)
Peveril of the Peak (Seat: Chinley)
Pitfour (Seat: Mintlaw) (two versions)
Plowden of Plowden (Seat: Strachur, Argyllshire)
Alan de Plunkenet

Hon. Sarah Ponsonby with Lady Eleanor Butler, one of the original ladies of Llangollen
Dr. John Radcliffe (Seat: Stony Stratford)
Dr. John Radcliffe (purchased in 1713, The Manor of Wolverton)
Amy Robsart
The Baron of Richmond, Yorks.
Robert de Ros
Rudyerd of Rudyard (See also K. Verses 1)
Thomas Rudyerd, 1626 (Seat: Rudyerd)
Hugh Saxey, 1638
The Skinners Arms
Stanley, King of Man
Stansfield of Eshott
Algernon Charles Swinburne 1837-1909. Buried at Bonchurch, I.W.
The Tennant Family
Thirsk, Lord of the Manor of
Thorne, Lords of the Manor of 1066-1347
Tournay, — Brockhill Park
The Tresham Family (Seat: Rothwell)
Tywyn of Deganwy
The Udny Arms (Seat: Newburgh-on-Ythan)
Umfreville — From an effigy in Hexham Abbey (Seat: Prudhoe-on-Tyne)
Dorothy Vernon (Early)
Dorothy Vernon (77966)
George Washington (Arms in Thrapston Church)
Josiah Wedgwood
Edward Leigh White, Esq. Bantry House, Castletown, Berehaven
Whitehead, Lord Mayor of, 1889
The Wynnstay Family (Seat: Ruabon)

D. Educational and Medical Establishments

Most of the items in this section are reasonably common, probably having been originally purchased by students of the establishments concerned from the local agent.

The majority would be worth + £3.00 – £5.00 with the exception of overseas establishments, which are valued at + £8.00

A number of Australian school arms have only recently come to light after being re-imported last year. All were originally stocked by Flavelle & Roberts, the Sydney agents until 1914.

Note: Some Universities are listed under Colleges and Schools because of the word 'College' in their titles.

A small range of Hospital Arms were produced, valued at + £5.00

1. UNIVERSITIES

Aberdeen University
Armidale School (N.S.W.)
Birmingham University (Founded by Sir Josiah Mason, Feb.23rd 1875)
Bristol University
Cambridge University,
and the following Colleges:
 Clare
 Corpus Christi
 Downing
 Emmanuel
 Fitzwilliam Hall
 Girton
 Gonville and Caius
 Jesus
 Kings
 Magdalene
 Pembroke
 Peterhouse (St.Peters)
 Queens
 St. Catherine's
 St. John's
 Selwyn
 Sidney Sussex(or Sydney)
 Trinity (College)
 Trinity Hall
Durham University
Durham University – St. John's Hall
Durham University – University College
Edinburgh University
Exeter University
Glasgow University
Hartley University – Southampton College
Harvard University, Boston, U.S.A., The Seal of
Kings College, London
Leeds University
Liverpool University
London University
Manchester – Victoria University
McGill University, Montreal
Oxford University,
and the following Colleges:
 All Souls
 Balliol
 Brazenose
 Christ Church
 Corpus Christi
 Exeter
 Hertford
 Jesus
 Keble
 Lincoln
 Magdalen
 Merton
 New (College)
 Oriel
 Pembroke

 Queen's
 St. Edmund Hall
 St. John's
 St. Peter's
 Somerville
 Trinity
 University
 Wadham
 Worcester
Queen's University, Kingston, Ontario, Canada
Reading University
St. Andrew's University (two versions)
Sheffield University
Sydney University
Trinity College, Dublin
University College of Bangor, North Wales
University College of Wales, Aberystwyth, Seal of
University College, London
University College, Reading
University of Leeds
University of North Wales, Bangor
Victoria University, British Columbia
Victoria University (Aust.)

2. COLLEGES and SCHOOLS

Abingdon College
Ackworth School
Adelaide Methodist Ladies College
Adelaide, Prince Alfred College
Adelaide, St. Peter's College
All Hallows School, Honiton
Archbishop Chichele's Grammar School, Higham Ferrars
Armstrong College, Newcastle-on-Tyne
Atherstone School, The Seal of
Avery Hill Training College, Eltham
Bala Theological College
Barnard Castle School
Bedford Grammar School
Bedford Modern School
Bedford School (Schola Bedfordiensis, 1552)
Berkhampsted School, 1541
Bingley College
Bishop Otter College, Chichester
Blairlooge School
Bloxham – All Saints' School
Blundell's School, Tiverton (Petrus Blundellus Fundator) (two varieties)
Bradfield College, Berks.
Brentwood School
Brewood Grammar School
Brighton College, (Motto in Greek)
Brighton Grammar School
Brisbane Boys' College
Brisbane – Somerville House High School for Girls
Camberley Royal Military College
Camberley Royal Staff College
Camborne Mining School
Central Foundation Schools of London
Chard School
Charterhouse School, Godalming
Cheltenham College
Cheltenham Dean Close School
Cheltenham – Jesus College
Cheltenham Ladies College
Cheltenham – Malvern College
Cheltenham Training College
Chester College
Chigwell School
Christ's Hospital (Blue Coat School), Horsham.
Cirencester College
Claremont Training College, Western Australia
Clifton College
College of Medicine, Newcastle-on-Tyne
Cranbrook School
Cranleigh School

University College of Wales,
Aberystwyth

Haileybury College

Girton College
(Cambridge)

Gonville & Caius
(Cambridge)

Worcester
(Oxford)

Oxford University (Named on base)

Jesus
(Cambridge)

Selwyn
(Cambridge)

Lord Williams's Grammar School,
Thame. 1575

St. Michael's College, Tenbury.

Sydney Sussex
(Cambridge)

Trinity
(Cambridge)

St. Mary's Hospital

London Hospital

Queens
(Oxford)

St. Johns
(Cambridge)

Croydon School
Culham College
Dollar Academy. Scotland
Dulwich College
Durham College of Medicine, Newcastle-on-Tyne
Durham School
Durham University College, City of
Edge Hill Training College
Edward VI Grammar School, Stratford-upon-Avon
Eton College (Floreat Etona)
Exeter College
Felsted School
Fishponds College
Floreat Wellingtonia (N.Z.)
Framlingham College
Fulneck Schools (Founded A.D. 1753)
Geelong (Australia) C.of E. Grammar School
Geelong (Australia) C.of E. Girls Grammar School
Geelong (Australia), The College
Geelong (Australia), Morongo Presbyterian Girls College
Giggleswick School
Godolphin School, Salisbury
Goole Secondary School
Greenwich Naval College
Greys College, Bloemfontein
Haileybury College
Hales Grammar School, Hertford
Harrow School
Heathfield School, Ascot
Highgate School
Higham Ferrars Grammar School
Hitchin Grammar School
Horsham School
Ironbridge School
Kimbolton Grammar School
King Alfred's Grammar School, Wantage
King James I Grammar School, Bishop Auckland
King's College, Colchester
Kings School, Bruton
Kings School, Canterbury
Kings School, Grantham
King William's College, Isle of Man
Leys School, Cambridge
Liverpool College for Girls, Huyton
Llandovery College
Lord Williams' Grammar School, Thame — 1575
Loughborough College
Magdalen College School, Brackley

Magdalen College School, Wayneflete. (Founded in 1459 by William of Wayneflete, Bishop of Winchester — also Magdalen College, Oxford)
Malvern College
Manchester Grammar School
Market Bosworth Grammar School
Marlborough College
Merchant Taylor's School, London
Middlesborough High School
Middleton College
Mill Hill School
Milton Abbas School
Mortimer College, Cleobury
Narvington College (Sydney)
Normal College, Biggleswade
North Eastern County School
North Sydney, Church of England Grammar School
North Wales Training College, Bangor
Oakham School
Ormond College, Melbourne
Oundle School
Owen's College, Manchester
Presbyterian Ladies' College, Melbourne
Queen Elizabeth's Grammar School, Crediton, Seal of
Repton School, 1557
Ripon School
Rondebosch Diocesan College, South Africa
Rossall School
Rugby, 1567 (Floreat Rugbaea)
Rugby — School House
St.Andrews College (Australia)
St. Bees Grammar School
St. Boswells
St.Hilda's School, Southport
St.Michael's College, Tenbury
St.Paul's College, Burgh
St.Paul's School, London
Sandwich Grammar School, 1563 A.D.
Saxey's School, Bruton, Somerset
Saxey Trade School
Sedburgh School
Shepton Mallet Grammar School
Sherborne School (Schol: Regal: Sherborne. Edward VI) (two versions)
Shrewsbury School
South African College. Founded 1829
South Wales Training College
The South Eastern Agricultural College, Wye

Southport Church of England Grammar School 'The Southport School'
Stanhope Girls' High School
Swansea School (Floreat Swansea)
Taunton School
Tenbury College
Theobald's Endowed School, Needham Market
Tiverton School
Tollington School
Tonbridge School. Founded in A.D.1553
Trinity College, Melbourne
United States Naval College
Uppingham School (two versions)
Victoria College, Stellenbosch, South Africa
Wellingborough Grammar School
Wellington College, Crowthorne
Wells Theological College. (Coll. Theo. Wellens A.D.1840)
Westminster School
Whitgift School (Archbishop Whitgift's School, (Croydon)
Winchester College (two versions)
Woodhouse Grove School, Apperley Bridge
Wycombe Abbey School

Guy's, London
The London
Middlesex, London
St. Bartholomew's, London
St. Cross, Winchester
St. Georges, London
St. Katherine's Ledbury (See also Bishop Hugh Foliot)
St. Marys, London
St. Thomas', London
University College Hospital, London
Westminster, London

1. ABBEYS, CATHEDRALS CHURCHES, FRIARIES, MONASTERIES, NUNNERIES, PRIORIES, CHAPELS

Abbeys, Friaries, Monasteries, Priories, Cathedrals, Churches, Dioceses and Sees are comparatively common and would not be worth any additional premium (with only a few exceptions).

Abbots, Bishops, Cardinals and Saints would attract + £3.00 – £5.00

(A) ABBEYS

Abergavenny
Amesbury
Amesbury (Seal of Abbey)
Bangor, Wales (Seal of Abbey A.D.1395)
Bardsey
Barking
Basingwerk, Greenfield
Bath
Battle
Beauchief
Beaulieu, 1204
Beverley
Blanchard, 1165
Bolton
Bruton
Buckfastleigh
Buckland (Nr. Yelverton) (Founded 1278)
Burnham, Bucks. (Founded 1165 A.D.)
Burnham (Founded 1165 A.D.)
Byland
Calder/Caldy
Cerne
Chatteris (Seal of Abbey.) (Founded 980 A.D. Dissolved 1538 A.D.)
Cirencester (First Coat)
Cirencester (Second Coat)
Cirencester (Third Coat)
Cleeve
Coggeshall
Colchester
Coverham, 1214 A.D.
Crowland (two versions, one with this legend:–
    The Abbey of Crowland, Founded by Ethelbald, King of Meina, A.D.729.
(Sometimes spelt Croyland)
Dieu La Cres (Leek)
Dorchester (two versions)
Dryburgh
Easby (two versions)
Evesham, Worcs.
Eynsham, Berks.
Faversham
Fountains
Furness (First Coat)
Furness – Second Coat
Glastonbury
Guisborough
Halesowen. 1215 – 1538
Hexham (see also p.49)
Horning
Hulton
Ilkley
Jervaulx, 1156 A.D.
Kelso
Knaresborough
Lacock
Leiston
Llanthony (Founded by Hugh de Lacy 1108)

Lymington
Margam
Malmesbury
Malvern
Melrose
Melrose, Ye Master Mason of.
Merevale
Milton
Missenden
Mount St.Bernard's (Coalville)
Mount St.Bernard's (Charnwood Forest)
Netley
Pershore
Reading
Richmond, Yorks.
Rivaulx
Romsey, The Seal of, Founded 907. (See also Commemoratives for 1907)
Rushen, Isle of Man
St. Albans
St. Bennets, Holme
Seascale
Sherborne
Shrewsbury
Skipton
Spalding
Tavistock
Tewkesbury (three versions)
Tintern
Torre
Tresco
Valle Crucis
Walden
Waltham (two versions)
Wenlock
West Dereham
Westminster
Whalley
Whitby
Whitby (St.Hilda and the Abbey Seal)
Winchcombe
Woburn
York, St.Mary's Abbey

B. CATHEDRALS

Ely
Hereford (Dean and Chapter)
Kildare, Ireland – Fourth Century Seal
Kildare, Ireland – Modern Seal
Lincoln
Peterborough
Ripon
St. Pauls, London, Seal of
Southwark (London)
Southwell
York Minster

C. CHURCHES

Beverley - The Collegiate Church of St. John
Headingley - St.Chad's Church 1356
Henfield - St.Peter's Church
London - St. Paul's Church, Lorriemore Square
Pensarn - Llanwenllwyfe Church
Southwell Minster - The Common Seal of the Chapter of the Collegiate Church of the Blessed Virgin Mary of Southwell
Stratford-on-Avon - "Shakespeare's Church"
Swaffham Church
Swaffham - St. Petyr and St. Pawll
Weardale - St. Johns Chapel
Windsor - St. George's Chapel

D. FRIARIES

Atherstone

E. MONASTERIES

Edington
Holland
Holme Cultram
Nantwich
Whalley

F. NUNNERIES

Amesbury, Seal of the Nunnery

G. PRIORIES

Barnstaple
Bicester
Bridlington (77966)
Carisbrooke, Ancient Seal of
Cartmel
Castle Acre
Colchester
Conishead
Dunmow (77966) (Specially made for the agents: Robus Bros., High Street, Dunmow)
Ely (two versions)
Faversham
Hexham
Holme Cultram
Hounslow
Kenilworth
Leigh, Essex
Lewes, 1078
Malvern
Norwich
Nuneaton
St. Osyth
Southwark
Stavordale, Wincanton
Tutbury
Tynemouth
Wenlock
Yeaveley

H. CHAPELS

St. George's, Windsor

2. ABBOTS, BISHOPS, CARDINALS and SAINTS

3. SEES, DIOCESES and BOARDS

Archbishop Abbot - Founder of Guildford Hospital, 1619.
Cardinal Beaufort (Winchester) Arms of, from the tomb in Winchester Cathedral.
Cardinal Beaufort (Winchester) Badge of
Cardinal Beaufort's White Hart
St. Thomas a'Becket (Archbishop of Canterbury) Dec.28th 1170
Bishop Coverdale, 1351
Bishop of Durham - the late Lord Crewe
Bishop Hugh Foliot of Ledbury, 1219-34. Founded St.Katherine's Hospital, 1232
Bishop Fox (Winchester) Arms of
Bishop Fox (Winchester) Badge of
Bishop Fox's Pelican
St. George
George (Saint) (Found on Blue Goss, q.v.)
Bishop Hooper
Bishop of Lincoln, Flag of
St. John the Baptist
Sherborne, Seal of the last Abbot of
Sherborne, Seal of the Abbot of, 1285-1310. Dug up in Sherborne (appears in red or black.)
Bishop Skirlaugh of Howden, 1406
   ("Bishop Skirlaugh indeed was good to his people, He built them a schoolhouse and heightened their steeple.")
James Stuart. Last Abbot of Dryburgh Abbey
Bishop Vesey, Arms of
Archbishop Whitgift
(Bishop) William of Wykeham
Cardinal Wolsey. Built Hampton Court, 1525. (Seat: Great House, Goff's Oak, East Molesey)

SEES

Bangor, Wales
Bath
Birmingham
Bristol
Canterbury
Carlisle
Chelmsford
Chester
Chichester
Colchester
Coventry, Ancient
Coventry
Dingwall
Douglas
Dromore
Durham
Ely
Exeter
Glastonbury
Gloucester
Hereford. A.D.1275
Hereford, Modern
Hereford Ancient
Hexham
Inverness
Isle of Man, Ancient
Lichfield
Lincoln
Liverpool
Llandaff
London
Longton
Man
Manchester
Moray Ross, Caithness
Newcastle-on-Tyne
Norwich
Orkney
Oxford
Peterborough
Ramsey, Isle of Man
Ripon
Rochester
St. Albans
St. Asaph
St. Davids
Salisbury
Southwark
Southwell
Sodor and Man
Sydney
Truro
Wakefield
Wells
Winchester
Worcester
York

DIOCESES

Leeds
Sydney (Australia)

MISCELLANEOUS

Hereford, Dean and Chapter

BURIAL BOARDS

Barking. Seal of the Burial Board of St. Margarets

See of St. Albans

See of Hereford. A.D.1275

Horning Abbey

Woburn Abbey

See of Oxford

St. George

Buckland Abbey, Nr. Yelverton

Colchester Abbey

Arms of St. Thomas A'Becket

Hugh Foliot. Bishop 1219-34.
Founded St. Katherine's
Hospital, Ledbury, 1232.

Seal of Abbey of Chatteris

St. Paul's Cathedral

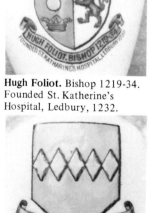

Conishead Priory

F. Miscellaneous

1. ORGANISATIONS

2. OTHER

Most of the items in this section are more desirable, simply because of their scarcity. All would be worth at least + £5.00 and some up to + £25.00

The values of League and International League of Goss collectors Arms will be found in "The Price Guide To Goss China". Whilst The Inns of Court would be worth + £15.00, The Sheffield Cutlers' Company & The Whitstable Dredgers Seal are comparatively common however and would only be worth + £2.00.

Ancient Order of Foresters, The
Association of the Men of Kent and Kentish Men, The
Band of Hope, The
Boy's Brigade, The
Boy's Brigade, The First Enfield Company of the
British South Africa Company
Church of England Temperance Society
Farmers of Aylesbury, The
Fishmongers' Arms, The
Golfers' Arms, The ("Fore!")
Golfers' Arms of Lundin Links, Scotland, The
Golfers of Oban, The
Golfers of Richmond, Yorks, The
Hendon & Cricklewood Rifle Club
Hereford Dean and Chapter
The Inns of Court:—
    Grays Inn
    Inner Temple
    Lincolns Inn
    Middle Temple
International League of Goss Collectors, The
Lancashire Aero Club
League of Goss Collectors, The
Liberal Christian League —
President: Rev. R.J.Campbell, M.A. 'We are members one of another'
National Commercial Temperance League of Business and Professional Men (Founded in 1891)
National Federation of Bakery Students Societies - Derby 1935 (N.F.B.S.S. Monogram)
Northampton - The Statute Merchants' Seal, 1319
Nottingham Merchants' Seal of
Okehampton Golfers Club
Our Dumb Friends' League
Portadown Town Commissioners 1883
Port of London Authority, The
Port St. Mary Commissioners, Isles of Scilly
Primrose League, The (Also "Peace with Honour") (two varieties)
Romney Marsh, Lords of the Level of, The
Sheffield - The Cutlers' Company
Sheffield - The Cutlers' Company (Arms elaborated)
Whitstable, The Seal of the Corporation of the Dredgers, 1793
York, The Merchant Adventurers of

Blazon - with explanation of Arms on reverse
Glastonbury - Ye olde Pilgrime's Inne Sign (Royal Arms of Edward IV)
Hythe Jurat's Seal, The
"Bow-Wow" (see Painswick — p. 29)
None of the undermentioned have been seen by the author and further verification is required. They are however, included for completeness.
Newdigate   The Holiday Camp
St. Teath, Banner of
The George Hotel
Wharton Hall (Seat: Kirkby Stephen) (two versions)

The League of Goss Collectors

International League of Goss Collectors

The Dumb Friends League

The Boys Brigade

Cat and Fiddle, Nr. Buxton

The Primrose League

Church of England Temperance
Society

Ancient Order of Foresters

St. John Ambulance Brigade

The Golfer's Arms

Decorations

G. Commemoratives

1887 Queen Victoria's Golden Jubilee. Crown, 'V' and ribbon with inscription. (Rd. No. 61464) + £30.00

1887 Queen Victoria's Golden Jubilee. Crown, 'V' and Garter Star (Rd. No. 60448) + £35.00

Note: While not being of a strictly commemorative nature, the designs of Rd. Nos. 61464 and 60448 were used again in 1888 and 1889, and may be found with these dates.

1887 Queen Victoria's Golden Jubilee. Four interlinked circles, the centre one carrying a crown and the surrounding ones the following words and details. (a) Top: 'Liberty', roses and leeks. (b) Lower Left: 'Loyalty' and thistles. (c) Lower Right: 'Legality' and shamrocks. (Rd. No. 78189) + £35.00

(**Note:** In the larger version, the background is white, while in the smaller, it is red on the outer circles and pale blue behind the crown.)

1888 Silver Wedding of the Prince and Princess of Wales – March 10th, 1888. Prince of Wales' feathers, entwined 'A and A', ribbon and inscription. + £50.00

1893 Wedding of Prince George and Princess May of Teck – 6th July, 1893. Crown, entwined 'G and M', ribbon with inscription. + £60.00

1896-7 Queen Victoria's Diamond Jubilee. Crown, 'V', ribbon with inscription '60th year of reign of our Beloved Queen' and 'R.I.'. + £25.00

1896-7 As above, but printed entirely in green. (This may be unique to the Canterbury agent, J. Abrahams, who published it.) + £40.00

1896-7 Queen Victoria's Diamond Jubilee. Black three-quarter profile transfer-print of the Queen, wearing small crown and Garter ribbon and Orders. Inscription: '60th Year of Reign 1896-7'. + £50.00

1896-7 Queen Victoria's Diamond Jubilee. A porcelain (a) rectangular panel, (b) shield shaped posy vase mounted on rectangular panel, and mounted in ornate brass surrounds, (a) in the form of a pipe-rack, and (b) in ornamental frame with scallop-shell shaped holder mounted beneath. Design:– 'Victoria D.G.' in ribbon scroll, 'Reg. Imp.', Crown, '1896 Annum LX Regnat 1897' in ribbon scroll, and 'Laud Deo'. + £20.00 (See Price Guide, p. 134)

Note: A whole range of brass items exists. All are of the same value.

1896-7 Queen Victoria's Diamond Jubilee. An unglazed parian bust of the Queen, wearing her small crown, and carrying the following inscription on the back: 'Memorial of 60th Year of Reign of Her Majesty, Victoria, R.I.' + £15.00 (See Price Guide, p.135)

1896-7 Queen Victoria's Diamond Jubilee. As above, but with the Queen wearing her 'mob-cap' – (several sizes)

(**Note:** Neither of the above busts were made specifically to commemorate the Golden Jubilee, both having first appeared some years previously. It is the inscription on the back which makes them commemorative items). + £15.00 (See Price Guide, p. 135)

1902 Coronation of Edward VII and Alexandra. A pair of unglazed parian busts of the King and Queen, on square plinths, and respectively 163mm and 175mm in height. Both bust bear the publication date – 7 May, 1901. (See Price Guide, p.137)

1902 Coronation of Edward VII and Alexandra. A pair of unglazed parian busts of the King and Queen, on socle (round) plinths, and respectively 133mm and 132mm in height. Both busts bear the publication date – 7 May, 1901. (see Price Guide, p. 137)

1902 Coronation of Edward VII and Alexandra. Crown, ornate 'E and A', (containing rose, shamrock, leek, and thistle) and ribbon bearing inscription, 'Edwardus VII. D.G. Britt. Omn. Rex. F.D. Ind. Imp. Crowned 26 June, 1902'. Also 9 August. Three sizes: 30mm £10.00, 55mm £15.00, 78mm £20.00

1910 Death of King Edward VII. Profile of King surrounded by laurel leaves and surmounted by Crown. The following inscription

appears in Gothic script either below the above decoration, or, if space does not permit, on the back of the item: 'Edward the Peacemaker. Born Nov. 9 1841. Ascended the Throne Jan 22 1901. Died May 6 1910'. + £25.00

1910 Death of King Edward VII. A three-handled loving cup carrying a profile of the late King in low relief on one panel, the Royal Arms of the late King together with the wording as above, on a second panel, and an appropriate coat-of-arms in the third panel. Price of complete piece £100.00

1911 Coronation of George V and Mary. Crown, ornate 'G and M', and ribbon bearing the inscription: 'George V. D.G. Britt. Omn. Rex. F.D. Ind. Imp. Crowned 22 June 1911'. (Rd. No. 573577) Three sizes: 29mm + £10.00, 55mm + £15.00, 80mm + £20.00

Items carrying this decoration were usually accompanied by a special descriptive leaflet, value £5.00, an example of which is shown here.

"GOSS" Coronation Porcelain.

This special registered Coronation Badge will not be reproduced after December 31st, 1911.

There will therefore be only a limited number of pieces made, which will gradually get scarcer through breakage, etc., and will therefore become more valuable in the future.

The devices on the five Bezants on the "G" each represent one of the great Colonies, viz., the Tiger for India, Beaver for Canada, Kangaroo for Australia, Lion for South Africa, and Apteryx (or Kiwi-Kiwi) for New Zealand.

The four on the "M" represent the United Kingdom, viz., Rose for England, Thistle for Scotland, Shamrock for Ireland, and Leek for Wales; and the May Blossom round the "M" refers to the Queen's pet name, "May."

1911 Investiture of the Prince of Wales. An unglazed parian bust of the Prince of Wales, in naval uniform, on a glazed column, overall height being 143mm. On the front of the column is a coloured pictorial of Carnarvon Castle with a yellow border, while on the back are the arms of Carnarvon. On the back of the bust is inscribed, 'Investiture of H.R.H. The Prince of Wales. Carnarvon Castle. 13 July 1911.' The publication date of this bust is 16 June 1911, and, without details of the Investiture on it, would not be considered a commemorative item. (See Price Guide, p. 137)

1935 Silver Jubilee of King George V and Queen Mary. Usually a beaker or mug, bearing the inscription, 'To commemorate the Silver Jubilee of King George V and Queen Mary', the dates 1910 and 1935 in a scroll at the foot, and all surrounded by floral scrolls. The only examples seen have all been on 'Goss-England' or 'Royal Buff' ware, that is, on Buff Pottery (not porcelain) in brown transfer. The reverse normally carries a pictorial in brown, not necessarily connected with the occasion. Specimens seen: Windsor Castle, Wells Cathedral and Alton Towers. + £15.00

1937 The (Non) Coronation of Edward VIII. (An attempt was made to withdraw these items from the market, but a considerable number had already been sold.) The Decoration comprised a portrait of the King in an oval frame surrounded by the Union Flag, two St. Andrews Crosses, and a Red Ensign. The whole is surmount-

George and Mary. Coronation 1911

Emperor Frederick (Death of, 1888)

Queen Victoria's Golden Jubilee 1887

Silver Wedding of The Prince and Princess of Wales 1888

ed by a crown, together with a scroll stating, 'May 12th. Coronation. 1937', and carrying below the King's portrait on ornate scroll with 'H.M. Edward VIII' with the rose, thistle and shamrock motif below it. + £15.00

1937 The (Non) Coronation of Edward VIII. A virtually round monochrome ash-tray (approx. 130mm in diameter), having centrally the flags of the Union and England, a crown, and the initials, 'E.R.' entwined. The rim bears the inscription, 'Edward VIII. Crowned May 12, 1937'. (This item is found in various colours including yellow and blue.) Value of item: £25.00

1937 Coronation of George VI and Elizabeth. The Decoration is as that detailed for the first of the Edward VIII items above except that portraits of George VI and Elizabeth replace that of Edward VIII and the scroll below states, 'George VI & Elizabeth'. + £15.00.

1937 Coronation of George VI and Elizabeth. Another decoration on beaker identical to that detailed for the 1935 Silver Jubilee of King George V. and Queen Mary, bearing the inscription 'To Commemorate the Coronation of King George VI and Queen Elizabeth' and the date 'May 12th 1937' split into two scrolls at the foot and surrounded by floral scrolls.(Royal Buff Pottery) + £15.00

1880. Robert Raikes – Centenary of Sunday Schools. (Profile head in roundel) + £40.00.

1884. Winchester Septencenterary. 1st Mayor Florence DeLunn 1184: 700th Thomas Stopher 1884. A colourful seal, very scarce. + £40.00.

1888. Death of Emperor Frederick – 'In Memory of the Heroic Emperor Frederick – died June 15. 1888'. Flagpole and flag at half mast, 'Gott Mit Uns 1870'. + £60.00

1888. Lord Fitzwilliam – Golden Wedding 10th Sept. 1888. + £40.00.

1891. Queen's visit to Derby. A taper milk jug bearing the Arms of Her Majesty the Queen and on the reverse the inscription "In Commemoration of the Queen's visit to Derby, May 21st 1891." + £40.00

1893. Winchester College Quincentenary. 500th Anniversary of Winchester College, founded by William of Wykeham A.D. 1393. (77966 Reg. Seal crest). Scarce. + £40.00

1894. Brierley Hill – Probably a regimental prize awarded at the army camp at Brierley Hill. + £30.00.

1895. Centenary of Death of Josiah Wedgwood. A Portland vase bearing the inscription on the base – 'Memorial of Josiah Wedgwood'. + £30.00. (To be perfectly correct the Arms should be those of Josiah Wedgwood, but almost all specimens bear other arms.)

1898. Death of W.E. Gladstone. The Arms of Gladstone, surrounded by the inscription – 'In memory of the Right Hon. W.E. Gladstone. Born 29 Dec. 1809. Died 19 May 1898'. + £20.00

1900. Frances Mary Buss Schools. Shield design comprising anchors, thistles, and ears of wheat over a ribbon banner. 'Jubilee Frances Mary Buss Schools'. + £40.00

1902. 'A Memento of Preston Guild 1902.' A Taper mug bearing the arms of Preston, and inscribed, 'The Right Hon. The Earl of Derby, K.G., Guild Mayor.' (The base carries the detail – 'Manufactured for Gibson and Howarth, Glass and China dealers to H.R.H. The Prince of Wales, Preston, by William H. Goss, Stoke-on-Trent.') + £30.00

1904. 50th Anniversary of Opening of Crystal Palace. A Grecian lady standing at an open doorway with lamb and helmet at her feet. Inscription – 'Crystal Palace' (in ribbon) and 'Opened 1854' Note without the opening date, this design would not be commemorative. Two sizes may be found, the larger, 47mm high + £20.00, being considerably rarer than the 35mm version. + £10.00

1905. Centenary of Death of Admiral Lord Nelson. Arms of Lord Nelson – 'Admiral Lord Nelson Centenary 1905'. S.+ £15.00, L. + £25.00

1906-1907. New Zealand International Exhibition Christchurch. (A black transfer print showing Exhibition Buildings and Gardens. Published by John Bates & Co., Worcester House, Christchurch, N.Z.). + £40.00.

1907. Romsey Abbey – 1000th Anniversary. 'Seal of Romsey Abbey. Founded 907. 1000 Anniversary Commemoration 1907'. + £10.00.

1910. Bournemouth Centenary. Three circular designs, interlinked, the top one containing the arms of the Borough of Bournemouth, and the lower two containing shields with the arms of Tregonwell and Tapps-Gervis. An inscription in a ribbon below reads, '1810 Bournemouth Centenary 1910'. Rd. No. 559519. + £20.00

1910. 30 Sept. THA? in script above the date, all in blue. The author does not know what this commemorates but it is probably a personal event.

1911. Alsager U.D.C. Coronation Mug. A taper mug, having the 'G & M' insignia, and on the reverse the arms of Alsager, together with the inscription: 'Alsager Urban District Council. W.Huntley Goss, Chairman'. Beneath the mug is printed, 'Given by the Chairman and Mrs. Goss'.

Coronation of George VI & Elizabeth 1937

Queen Victoria's Golden
Jubilee 1887 Garter Star

Queen Victoria's Golden
Jubilee 1888

Queen Victoria's Golden
Jubilee 1889 Garter Star

Queen Victoria's Diamond
Jubilee 1896–7

Wedding of Princess May of
Teck and George V

Queen Victoria's Golden
Jubilee. 'Liberty, Loyalty,
Legality'.

Edward The Peacemaker (Death of, 1910)

Pictorial View of Queen
Victoria (Diamond Jubilee)

Coronation of Edward VIII
1937

(The above is of particular interest as it was W. Huntley Goss who directed the firm of W.H. Goss from 1912 until its final days). + £30.00

1911. Whitstable Coronation Mug. A straight-sided mug having the 'G & M' insignia on side and on the reverse the inscription 'Presented at Whitstable on the occasion of the Coronation of their Majesties King George V. and Queen Mary'. + £30.00

1911. Thurlow Presentation Beaker. A beaker having the 'G & M' insignia and the following inscription on the base: 'With the compliments of Messrs. G. Thurlow & Sons Ltd.'. (This was an engineering firm in Stowmarket.) + £35.00

1911. Chesham Bois Coronation Mug. A 73mm Taper mug having crossed Union Jacks, and a crown over a rose. 'Fear God and Honour the King' – 'Chesham Bois June 22, 1911. Coronation day of King George V' – 'Presented by Mr. & Mrs. Cecil Cave-Brown-Cave. + £35.00

1919. Alsager Peace Mug. The normal 'Peace' motif – and on the reverse – the Alsager U.D.C. Coat-of-Arms and 'Given by Thomas F. Owen (Chairman) & Mrs. Owen'. + £30.00

1919. Denton Peace Beaker. A Taper beaker bearing the arms of Denton and Haughton, 'Presented by the Urban District Council of Denton and Haughton.' + £35.00

1919. Felixstowe Peace Mug. A Taper mug, bearing the Arms of Felixstowe and around them the wording, 'Peace Celebrations 1919'. + £30.00

1920. Milton Regis Presentation Mug. The normal Taper mug with rim, bearing the Arms of Milton Regis, with base inscription: – Milton Regis Urban District Council, Chairman, Walter J. Elgar, Esq., J.P., C.C. These mugs were presented at a tea and entertainment on October 1st 1920 to the Children of Milton Regis whose fathers gave their lives in the services of their country during the Great War 1914-18.
A tag (3" x 1.8") accompanied each of these mugs and was suitably inscribed to each recipient. The one attached to the specimen we have seen reads as follows: – 'Milton Regis. Town Committee for Entertaining the Returned Soldiers and Sailors. This Mug Was Presented to Victor Russell at a Tea and Entertainment on October 1st 1920, to the Widows and Children of Soldiers and Sailors of Milton Regis who lost their lives in the services of their country during the Great War 1914-18. Walter R. Elgar, Chairman.'
(To follow this particular item right through its history, the back of the tag bears the handwritten instruction: – 'This and the other Peace Jug to be given to Joy and June Clout in memory of their cousin Victor Russell who died October 26, 1926.') + £40.00

1920. Windleshaw Chantry. A model of Windleshaw Chantry, carrying the inscription on its base – 'A Present from Lowe House New Church Bazaar. 1920', and bearing the arms: En Dieu est Mon Esperance. Value of item £150.00. (Price Guide p.86)

1921. St.Peter's Church, Carmarthen, 17th September 1921 on large Bagware teapot with Arms of Carmarthen on the obverse. + £15.00

1922. 'A Momento of Preston Guild, 1922'. The Arms of Preston, and the inscription: 'Henry Astley-Bell, Esq., J.P., Guild Mayor'. + £30.00

1923. Alsager and District Fur & Feather Society Show 1923. Class's 19-25 Hen (found printed on base of large Japan Ewer, bearing arms of Alsager & Cheshire). + £20.00.

1923. Jubilee of Hebburn Church. (See also Transfer prints – U.K.) A sepia pictorial of the church, with the inscription: – 'The Jubilee of St. Andrew's Presbyterian Church, 1923'. + £35.00

1923. Opening of London Road Recreation Ground Lake, Derbyshire. Inscription: – 'London Road Recreation Ground Lake – Opened 29 September 1923'. + £40.00

1924. Lytham St. Anne's Xmas Treat. A 4" mug carrying the Lytham St. Anne's Arms, and the following inscription on the back: – 'Childrens Treat. Xmas 1924. Organized by St. Anne's R.A.O.B.' (Royal Ancient Order of Buffaloes.) + £40.00

1926. Wesleyan Methodist Church, Askew Road, London, W12.
1866 – 1926. Diamond Jubilee. A black transfer print of the church, and the above inscription. + £35.00

1926. Boy's Brigade Camp. The Badge of the Boys' Brigade surrounded by a laurel wreath and the inscription 'A Souvenir From 1926 Camp'. Black + £15.00 or more rarely brown + £20.00.
(Note: – The Boys' Brigade had a regular annual camp at Whitecliff Bay, in the Isle of Wight, and it has been confirmed that Goss souvenirs were sold over a period of some six years. Those bearing the simple inscription 'A Souvenir from Whitecliff Camp' would be difficult to date, but they can safely be assumed to come from the years 1926 to 1932. + £10.00)

1927. Boys' Brigade Camp. As above but dated 1927. + £15.00

1927. Juvenile Foresters Society of Burton-on-Trent. Jubilee 1927. + £35.00

1927. Alsager and District Fur and Feather Society Show 1927 Class 29–51 Best Hen, + £20.00

1928. Alsager and District Fur and Feather Society Show 1928 Class 16–27 Best Norwich. (These two inscriptions found on the base of large models) + £20.00

1931. Boys' Brigade Camp. The Badge of the Boys Brigade, as for 1926 but dated 1931. + £20.00.

1932. Boys' Brigade Camp. As for 1931, but dated 1932. + £20.00
Boys' Brigade. Souvenir of 'Ascog Camp', 'Gorbals District'. + £20.00

OTHER

London Cycle Club (commemorating twenty-five years of the Club) + £30.00

Memento of Preston Guild 1922

National Federation of Bakery Students Societies. Derby 1935 (Monogram)

London Road Recreation Ground Lake. Opened 29 September, 1923.

Bournemouth Centenary 1810–1910

Alsager U.D.C. W. Huntley Goss Chairman

Whitstable Coronation Mug 1911

Alsager U.D.C. Given by Thomas F. Owen (Chairman) & Mrs. Owen.

Felixstowe Peace Celebrations 1919 (on a Taper Mug)

Seal of Romsey Abbey 1907 1000 Anniversary

National Commercial Temperance League of Business and Professional Men. Founded 1891

T.H.A. (?) 30 Sept. 1910 A rare Personal Commemorative.

Memento of Preston Guild 1902

A Souvenir from Whitecliff Camp

Death of The Rt. Hon. W. E. Gladstone 1898

Four Flags of the Allies (with Russian Naval Flag)

Seven Flags of the Allies. ' L'Union Fait La Force Eendracht Maakt Macht'

Rare Dish Commemorating the German Attack on Scarborough 1914

Peace 1919

U.S. & G.B. Flags. 'Unity is Strength'

Seven Flags of the Allies

Four Flags of the Allies

1900 South African (Boer) War. The Union Jack and the White Ensign crossed and surmounted by a Royal Crown, with the Royal Standard Shield and 'South Africa 1900' below. + £60.00

1900 South African War. A British soldier, holding the Union Jack and trampling on the Boer Flag. Two sizes: 70mm + £30.00, 100mm + £40.00

1914-18 Two Flags of the Allies. Flags of Great Britain and U.S.A. with an anchor between them. 'Unity is Strength'. (Possibly this decoration dates from 1917 commemorating the entry of the United States into the War.) + £30.00

1914-18 Two Flags – as for Franco-British Exhibition (1908), but omitting reference to the Exhibition (Rd. No. 522181). (This decoration is often accompanied by the linked standards of Great Britain and France – Britain being spelled incorrectly on all models seen – 'Britian'). + £10.00

1914-18 Four Flags (Great Britain, France, Belgium, Russia – the Russian Naval Flag, a blue diagonal cross on a white background, being incorrectly used initially). + £10.00

1914-18 Four Flags (Great Britain, France, Belgium, Russia – having the correct Russian Flag, namely with white, blue, and red horizontal stripes. + £10.00

1914-18 Four Flags, 'plus one', or 'plus two'. The above four-flag decoration was often placed on larger models, and one or two additional single flags were added to fill up otherwise blank spaces. (One specimen to hand shews additionally the flags of Servia and Japan). + £15.00 for either or both flags.

1914-18 Six Flags. The named flags of Great Britain, France, Russia, Japan, Servia and Belgium around the perimeter of a plate surrounding this verse: –

'To Cook a German Sausage
Cook on a British kitchener,
Use a Japan enamelled sauce-pan,
Grease well with Russian tallow,
Flavour with a little jellicoe,
Servia!! Up with French capers,
And Brussells Sprouts.'

(Occasionally the word 'sausage' is omitted, the wording lowered, and a coat-of-arms inserted). 150mm + £100.00.
Six Flags surrounding a coat-of-arms: 150mm + £30.00, 250mm + £50.00

1914-18 Seven Flags – on vases, etc. (Great Britain, France, Belgium, Servia, Russia, Japan and Italy). + £15.00

1914-18 Seven Flags – as above, except that instead of naming the countries, this piece bears the inscription, 'L'Union Fait La Force – Eendracht Maakt Macht'. + £50.00 (This variation would have been for sale in Allied Europe, the particular specimen to hand bearing the Publisher's name – F.B. Den Boer, Middelburg.)

1914-18 Seven Flags. Seven named flags around the perimeter of a plate – Great Britain, France, Russia, Japan, Servia, Belgium and Italy, **or** U.S. of America. + £30.00

1914-18 Seven Flags. A 'three-quarter' shaped plate, specially commissioned by J.G. Nairn of Southport. Having six flags (Japan, France, Russia, Belgium, Serbia and Montenegro) around the perimeter, and the Union Jack central. It bears two inscriptions: – (a) 'Up, Ye Sons of England, And Wreak Vengeance on the Baby-Killers of Scarborough' around the edge, and (b) 'We Follow You In Our Daily Thoughts On Your Certain Road To Victory. George R.I. Dec. 5th 1914' around the Union Jack. Item priced at £200.00

1914-18 Eight Flags, having eight named flags (France, Russia, Italy, Serbia, Japan, Montenegro, Great Britain and Belgium) around the perimeter with a heraldic lion in the centre. Inscription 'L'Union Fait La Force – Eendracht Maakt Macht'. + £70.00

1915 Waterloo Memorial (presumably Centenary Commemorative). Two sizes: 30mm + £15.00, 50mm + £20.00.

1919 Peace, 1919 – An angel standing on a plinth surrounded by a laurel wreath, carrying the names of the Allied Countries – Greece, Portugal, Japan, Belgium, U.S. America, Serbia, Montenegro, Rumania, Italy, France, Gt. Britain and Dominions. (This decoration is found in two sizes, the larger, 52mm in height + £15.00 being scarcer than the 36mm version + £10.00).

1919 Peace – A design for large plates, being an elaboration of the above. An angel, standing on a plinth surrounded by the Flags of the Allies and above the names of Great Britain and her Dependencies and Allies. A laurel wreath surrounds the Flags and contains the names of famous war leaders – Haig, Foch, Joffre, Beatty, Tyrwhitt, Jellicoe, Birdwood, Horne, Rawlinson, Byng, Currie, Plumer, Maude, Marshall, Cavan, Allenby, D'Espercy, Dia, French, Monash, Pershing and Robertson. Value of item £250.00

see p.9 and frontispiece.

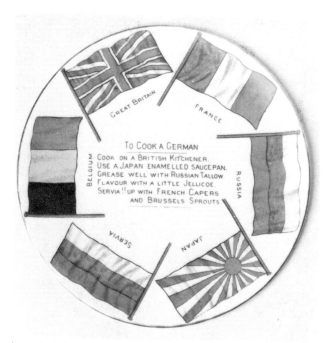

To Cook A German (Sausage) Plate

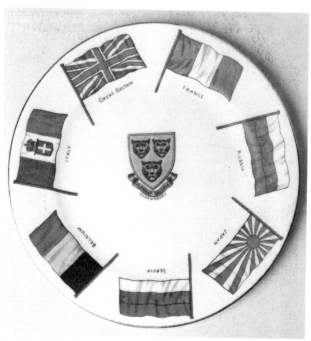

Teaplate 200mm Emblazoned with Seven Flags of the Allies
(The U.S. of America Flag sometimes replaces the Russian)

Waterloo Memorial 1815.
(Presumably Centenary Commemorative)

South Africa 1900 (Boer War)

1905. Dominion Fair. New Westminster, B.C. (Canada). + £25.00

1908 Franco-British Exhibition 1908. The crossed flags of France and Britain, with clasped hands in wreath of flowers and laurel leaves, 'Amitie Friendship'. Rd. No. 522181. + £10.00

Some versions of this commemorative design carry on the reverse the Standards of Britain and France, the word 'Britain' invariably spelled incorrectly 'Britian'.

A variation of the above may be found without reference to the Exhibition. It may be a 'resurrection' of the design for use during the 1914-18 War. + £10.00

1909.'Africa and The East' Exhibition. Shield, with sun's rays in top half, with three appropriate figures over named maps of Africa, China and India, 'Africa and The East' 1909. + £15.00. Rarely inscribed 'Birmingham 1910'. + £20.00

1910.'Festival of Empire – Crystal Palace 1910'. Britannia and another holding hands, a lion seated between them. + £10.00

1911.Festival of Empire 1911 – Crystal Palace Opened 1854. Design as above, except crown added between heads of two figures. + £10.00

1914.Missionary Exhibition – Tottenham & Wood Green 1914. The two sides of the Globe with hand across equator reading: 'From Sea to Sea'. + £25.00

1924.British Empire Exhibition. A stylized lion design on a shield above a ribbon banner inscribed: 'British Empire Exhibition, Wembley 1924'. (There are two sizes of this decoration, the larger 57mm high, + £15.00 being considerably rarer than the smaller, + £10.00

1924.British Empire Exhibition (See also Pictorial Items.) The following pictorial items were produced expressly in connection with the exhibition:–

The Gardens. B.E.E. 1924 (Brown) + £20.00 – £25.00

H.M. Government Buildings. B.E.E. 1924 (Brown) + £20.00 – £25.00

North Cascade and Tower. B.E.E. (Late colour). + £15.00

The Indian Pavilion. B.E.E. 1924 (Brown) + £20.00 – £25.00

Old London Bridge. B.E.E. 1924 (Brown) + £20.00 – £25.00

1924-25. Rose, Thistle, Shamrock and Leek – All separate decorations on a single piece undated but associated with the B.E.E. at Wembley.

1924-25. Rose, Thistle, Shamrock and Leek entwined, and beneath, in a ribbon scroll 'Wembley'. Some specimens bore 'A Present From' above the design. Two sizes are found, the larger, 55mm high excluding 'A Present From' being considerably rarer. + £10.00 and + £20.00 respectively. (Note although this decoration is not dated it is found in conjunction with the 1924 and 1925 designs and must therefore be regarded as of that date.)

1925.British Empire Exhibition. The stylized lion on the shield, as for 1924, but dated 1925. Small and large size £10.00 and £15.00 respectively.

1925.British Empire Exhibition. A stylized model of a seated lion on a plinth, carrying the above 1925 decoration. (No specimen has been found dated 1924.) Item valued at £150.00

1938.Empire Exhibition. Scotland. A Heraldic rampant lion in red, overchecked in white with the inscription below:–

Empire Exhibition. Scotland 1938. (This motif is found in two sizes, the larger being much the rarer.) + £10.00 and + £15.00 respectively.

Note: – It would appear that there were two sets of these designs, varying in inscription. Those entitled 'Olympic Games' also carried 'London' and '1908' below the decoration whereas those entitled 'Olympian Games' carried no reference as to location or date. The designs used were:–

'Discobolos'. Rd. No. 522178

'Victory Driving a Chariot'. Rd. No. 522179

'Hermes and Dionysos'. Rd. No. 522180

'The Boxers'. Rd. No. 522182

'Victory'. Rd. No. 522183

These designs appeared in two sizes, the larger being considerably rarer. + £30.00 and + £40.00 respectively.

(Note: The 'missing' registered number 522181 was used for the 'Franco – British Exhibition', which was also held in 1908.)

The Boxers

Hermes & Dionysos

British Empire Exhibition
Wembley 1925

British Empire Exhibition
Wembley 1924

Victory

Discobolos

Festival of Empire. Crystal
Palace 1910

Crystal Palace Opened 1854
Festival of Empire 1911

Victory Driving a Chariot

Crystal Palace Opened 1854

1924-5. Although undated,
associated with the B.E.E.
at Wembley.

Tottenham & Wood Green
Missionary Exhibition 1914

Franco-British Exhibition 1908

71

H. Transfer Printed Pictorial Views

These were produced as the pre-decessors of the picture post-card from about 1880 right up until 1938. Examples produced after 1929/30 when the factory changed hands are W.H. Goss. England and are termed here 'late'.

All the items mentioned here are transfer printed only, i.e. no painting except colour-washing has been applied after the transfer has been affixed. Items with some painting but which would appear to be found under this heading may be found in (B) N. Other Decorations.

Brown (sepia) and black transfers are the most common and would add around £15.00 on a small piece, £20.00 on a medium piece and £25.00 on a larger important item.

Green, red, blue and early colour transfers would add some £25.00 to a small piece, £30.00 to a medium and £40.00 to a large piece.

Sometimes two or more transfers are found on the same piece. Add 20% − 40% to the values listed in these cases. The value of late colour transfers is + £10.00 − £20.00.

A series of transfers were made for the Canadian market: these are all rare and range from + £35.00 − £60.00 according to size. The colour of the majority is brown.

A number of Empire and Foreign views were also listed, which are valued the same as the Canadian series.

This list has been compiled partly from 55 copper plates used for printing the transfers and three surviving Goss pattern books now in the possession of Allied English Potteries Ltd. Those transfers which have no colour noted in the right hand column are probably taken from these pattern books. Since the first edition some 50 of these transfers have been seen and their colour(s) have been noted in this edition. This proves beyond reasonable doubt that all the transfers in the pattern books do exist and are just waiting to be found!

The remainder of the items listed have been taken from various sources, the main one being the list published by the Goss Collectors' Club a few years ago. A number of collectors have also contributed details from their own collections. Where no colour is stated for a particular item, this could mean that the details were taken from the original copperplates rather than from actual specimens seen by the author.

Abbotsbury	The Tithe Barn	Black
Aber	The Falls	Brown
Aberdeen	Castle Street	Brown
Aberdovey		Colour, Black
Aberdovey	Church	Red
Abergavenny	Castle	Black
Abergavenny		Black
Aberystwyth		Brown
Aberystwyth	The Devil's Bridge	Black, Brown
Aberyswyth	The College	Black, Colour
Adderley	The Church and Rectory	
Albreath	The Castle	
Alloa	New Town Hall	Black
Alloway, Ayr	Burns' Monument and Tea Gardens	
Alloway, Ayr	Burns' Cottage	Brown, Black Colour (late)
Alloway, Ayr	Burns Monument, "Banks o' Doon"	Brown, Black
Alnmouth	Alnmouth and the beach from Church Hill	
Alnwick	The Castle	Brown
Alton Towers		Colour, Brown, Brown (late)
Alton Towers	The Gardens	Brown
Ambleside	St.Mary's Church	Brown
Andover	The Church	Colour, Black
Andover	High Street	Black, Colour
Apley	The Hall	Colour
Appleby	The Castle	
Arbroath	The Abbey	Black
Arbroath	The Castle	Black
Ardrosson		Black, Brown
Arundel		Black
Arundel	The Castle	Brown, Colour, Black
Ashbourne	The Church	Colour
Ashburton	The Church	Colour
Ashby-de-la-Zouch	The Castle	Colour
Ashford	The Church	Black
Astbury	The Church	Black
Audley End		Black
Axminster	St. Mary's Church	Black
Aylesbury	The Clock Tower and Market Square	Brown
Aylsham	Blickling Hall − The Birthplace of Ann Boleyn	Brown
Ayton	The Castle	
Ayton	The High Street	
Bagillt	St.Mary's Church	
Bakewell	Haddon Hall	Red, Black
Bala	The Church	Brown
Bala	The Lake	Brown
Balmoral	The Castle	Colour
Bamburgh	The Castle	Black, Brown
Bamburgh	St.Aidan's Church	Colour, Black
Bamburgh	Grace Darling's Monument	Green, Black
Bamburgh	Grace Darling's Coble	Black
Banbury	Church and Vicarage	
Banbury	The Cross	Brown
Banchory	Brig o' Teugh	

Great Marlow

Town Hall, Portsmouth

H.M.S. Victory, Portsmouth

Coming Down Hill, Malvern

Lincoln Imp

Chepstow Castle

Castel S. Angelo. Rare foreign View

John Keble

Banchory	The High Street	
Bangor	The Cathedral	Red
Barmouth		Black, Colour
Barmouth	The Bridge	Black
Barnard	The Castle	Black, Grey, Colour
Barry Dock	The Harbour	
Basing	Basing House, Time of Siege, 1643	Brown, Red
Basing	The Castle	Brown
Basingstoke	The Town Hall	
Bath	Pulteney Bridge and St.Michaels Church	Black
Bath	The Abbey from the N.E.	Colour, Black
Bath	The Pump Room	
Bath	The Royal Crescent	Black
Bath	Victoria Park	Colour, Black
Battle	The Abbey	Colour, Black
Beaumaris	The Castle Gate	
Beccles		Colour
Beccles	The Church	Colour
Bedale	The Church	Brown
Beddgelert	Gelert's Grave	
Bedford	Parish Church	Brown
Bedford	St.Mary's Church	Brown
Bedruthan	Queen Bess Rock	
Ben Rhydding	Cow & Calf Rocks	
Berwick-upon-Tweed	The Three Bridges	
Bettwys-y-coed	The Fairy Glen	Black
Beverley	The Minster	Brown
Bewdley		Black, Colour
Bewdley	Blackstone Rock	Black
Bewdley	The Bridge	
Bewdley	Quay and Bridge	Colour, Brown
Bewdley	Ribbesford Avenue	Brown
Biddulph	Old Hall	Black
Biggar	The Main Street	Brown, Colour
Biggleswade	St. Andrew's Church	Brown
Biggleswade	The Market Square	Brown
Birchington	Alden Church	Black
Birmingham	St.Cuthbert's Well	
Bisham	The Abbey	
Bisham	The Church	Black, Brown
Bishops Stortford	Parish Church	Black
Bishops Waltham	The Palace	Black
Blackpool	The North Pier	Brown
Blackpool		Brown
Blackpool	Rough Sea	
Blackpool	The Tower	Brown
Blairgowrie	Craig Hall	Black
Blarney	The Castle	Black, Green
Blenheim	The Palace	Brown, Colour
Blockley	The Church	
Bodiam	The Castle	Brown, Black
Boddam	Buchan Ness Lighthouse	
Bognor	Craigwell House	
Bognor	The Esplanade	Black
Bolton	The Abbey (General View)	Black
Bolton	The Abbey (West Front)	Red. Brown
Bonchurch	The Pond	Black
Boscombe	The Chine and Rustic Bridge	Colour
Boscombe	The Flower Gardens	Colour
Boscombe	The Pier Approach	
Boston	The Church	Brown
Bournemouth	The Gardens (Gardens & Church)	Colour, Black
Bournemouth	The Gardens (Tree-lined Walk)	Colour
Bournemouth	The Pavilion	Colour
Bournemouth	Undercliff Drive	Colour
Bournemouth	From West Cliff	Colour
Bournemouth	The Pier Approach	Colour
Bournemouth	Invalids Walk	Colour
Bournemouth	Pier and West Cliff	Colour
Bowmore, Islay		
Bowness	Belle Isle, Bowness and Windermere Lake	
Bowness, Windermere	View of the Bay	Black
Braemar	The Castle	Brown
Brampton	Lanercoat Gateway	
Brecon	The Priory Church	Colour
Brecon	The Castle	Brown
Bridgnorth	High Rock	Black
Bridgnorth	High Street	Black
Bridgnorth	The Severn	Black
Bridlington	The North Pier, Bridlington Harbour	
Bridport	St. Mary's Church	Colour
Brighton	The Beach and Sea-Front from the Palace Pier	
Brighton	King's Road looking East	
Brighton	The Metropole Hotel	Red
Brighton	The Palace Pier	
Broadstairs	Two views of the Beach	Black
Broadstairs	York Gate	Black
Broadstairs	View through York Gate	Black
Broadway Beacon, Worcs.	The Tower	Brown
Broadway	The Tower	Brown
Brodick	The Bay and Goat Fell	Brown
Builth	The Bridge	Black
Burford	The Church	Brown, Black
Burnham	The Church	
Burnham-on-Sea		Black
Burns, Robert	(Bust of)	Colour (late)
Buxton	The Cat and Fiddle Inn	Colour, Grey, Brown
Buxton	The Crescent	Brown
Buxton	The Devonshire Hospital	
Buxton	The Gardens and Waterfall	
Buxton	The Pavilion	
Buxton	St. Anne's Well	Brown
Byland	The Abbey	Brown
Caerphilly	The Castle	Brown
Callander and Ben Ledi	Bridge of	Colour
Calne	The Church	Black
Calne	Town Hall	Black
Cambridge	King's College	Brown
Cambridge	Trinity College	
Campbeltown	From Gallows Hill	Black
Canterbury	The Cathedral	Colour (late), Red, Black
Canterbury	College	Black

Weymouth

St. Clement's, Sandwich

Wilberforce House, Hull

St. Aidan's Church, Bamburgh

Canterbury	The West Gate	Black, Colour
Cardiff	The Castle	Black, Red
Carew	The Castle	
Carisbrooke, I.o.W.	The Castle	Black, Colour, Brown
Carisbrooke, I.o.W.	The Inn	
Carlisle	The Castle	
Carnarvon	The Castle	Red, Black or coloured in yellow border.
Cartmel	The Church	Red, Brown
Cartmel	Cartmel Hill	Black
Castleton	Peveril Castle	Brown
Chalfont St.Giles	Milton's Cottage	
Chard	The Church	Black
Charlbury	Ye Olde Market House	
Chatsworth	The House	Black, Red, Brown
Chelmsford	The Cathedral	Black
Chelmsford	The Church	
Cheltenham	Pitville Spa	Colour, Red
Cheltenham	The Promenade	Black, Colour (late)
Chepstow	The Castle	Black, Colour
Chester	The Cathedral	Brown, Colour (late)
Chester	The Cross	
Chester	The Globe	
Chester	The Phoenix, or King Charles' Tower	Brown
Chester	St. John's Priory Ruins	Brown
Chesterfield	The Parish Church	Brown
Chesterfield	The Parish Church from the S.W.	Brown
Chichester	The Cathedral	Colour, Black
Chichester	The Market Cross	Colour (late)
Chiddingfold	The Village Pond	Brown, Colour
Chillingham	The Deer in the Castle Park	Black
Chillingham	The Wild Cattle (2 examples)	Colour, Black
Chippenham	High Street	Black
Chippenham	Market Place	Black
Chirk (North Wales)	Castle Gates	Brown
Chirk	Chirk Castle, N.Wales	Brown
Chirnside		
Christchurch		Red, Black, Brown
Cirencester	The Church	Black
Cirencester	The Market Place	Colour (late)
Cirencester	R.A. College	Black
Clachan, Strachur		
Clacton-on-Sea	View of Life-boat House	Black
Clacton-on-Sea	Marine Parade West	Colour
Clacton-on-Sea	The Pier	Colour
Clevedon	The Beach	Black, Brown
Clevedon	Green Beach	Black, Brown
Clifton	The Suspension Bridge	Black
Clovelly	The High Street	
Clovelly	The Hunt	Colour (late)
Clovelly	Up along Clovelly.	Black, Red
Colchester	The Castle	Colour (late)
Colchester	The Pageant 1909	
Colchester	St. Botolph's Priory	
Coleford	The Church Tower and Market Place	
Colwyn Bay	The Dingle	Colour
Colwyn Bay		Colour
Colyton	The Church	Colour
Congleton		Black
Conway	The Castle	Red, Black & Blue
Corfe Castle	The Castle (2 varieties)	
Cork	Patrick Street	Black
Coventry	The Grey Friars Hospital	Brown
Coventry	Lady Godiva	Brown
Coventry	Peeping Tom	Brown
Coventry	The Three Spires	Black
Cowes	The Marine Parade, West Cowes	Colour, Black
Cowes (East)	Osborne House	Black, Brown
Cowes (West)	Marine Parade	Black, Colour
Cranbrook	The Church	
Criccieth	The Castle	Brown, Black
Cromer		
Crowborough	All Saints' Church	Black
Crowborough	The Cross	Black
Cupar	Crossgate	Black
Dalbeattie	Victoria's Jubilee Memorial	Black
Darlington	Parish Church	Colour
Darlington	No. 1 Locomotive	Brown
Darlington	St. Cuthbert's Church	Black, Red
Dartmouth	The Butterwalk	Black, Colour
Dartmouth	The Castle	Black, Colour, Brown
Dartmouth	The Mouth of the Dart	
Dartmouth	View from Warfleet Creek	
Dawlish	The Lawns	Black
Deal	The Castle	Red
Deeside	Dinnet Bridge	
Denbigh	The Castle	
Derby		Black
Derby	The Free Library	Black
Derwentwater		Colour
Derwentwater	Friar's Crag, Keswick	Colour (late)
Derwentwater	Keswick	Black
Devizes	The Market Cross	Black, Brown
Devizes	The Market Place	Brown
Dewsbury	Parish Church	Brown
Doncaster	The Parish Church	Brown
Doncaster	St.George's Church	Brown
Doncaster	Racecourse during races	Brown
Dorchester	High Street	
Dorking	High Street	Black
Dorking		Black
Douglas	Tower of Refuge	Black
Doune	The Castle	Black
Doune	The Castle from N.E.	Black
Doune	Castle from S.E.	Black
Dovedale	Entrance to	
Dovedale	Stepping Stones	Colour (late)
Dover	The Castle	
Dovercourt		
Downham Market	St.Edmund's Church	Brown
Downham Market	St.Nicholas Church	Brown
Droitwich	Dodder Hill Church	Brown
Droitwich	The High Street	Black, Red
Droitwich	Hadsor House	Black, Brown
Droitwich	The Raven	Black, Colour
Dryburgh	St.Mary's Aisle, Dryburgh Abbey	Colour (late)

Old Town, Matlock

First and Last House, Land's End

Barnard Castle

Sanctuary Knocker, Durham Cathedral.

Place	Subject	Colour
Dumfries	Burns' Mausoleum	
Dumfries	Sweetheart Abbey	Green, Dark Green, Orange, Grey, Brown
Dunbar	The Swimming Pond	Black, Brown, Red, Colour (late)
Dunfermline	The Abbey	
Dunstable	Priory Church	Brown
Dunster	Market House & Castle	Brown
Dungarven	Harbour	Black, Green
Durham		Black
Durham	The Cathedral	Black, Red
Durham	The Dun Cow, Durham Cathedral	Black
Durham	The Sanctuary Knocker on the North Door of the Cathedral	Black, Brown
Dwygyfylchi	The Village	Brown, Black
Eastbourne	The Grand Parade	Black
Eastbourne	The Pier	
Eastbourne	Splash Point	
Eastbourne	St. Mary's Church	
Eastbourne	View from the Wish Tower	
Eaton	The Hall	
Ebbw Vale	The Old Arch	
Edinburgh	The Castle with the Scottish National War Memorial and Earl Haig's Statue	
Edinburgh	Scott's Monument, Princes Street	Black, Brown
Egremont, Cumberland	The Castle Ruins	
Eilian Bay		
Ellastone	Adam Bede	Brown
Ely	The Cathedral	
Erdington	The Abbey	Brown
Evesham	The River and the Bridge	
Evesham	The Church	Brown
The Vale of Evesham	The Monument	Brown
Exeter	The Cathedral, from the West	Brown (on Royal Buff), Black
Exeter	The Cathedral	Black, Brown
Exeter	The Guildhall	
Exford	The Deer	
Eyam	The Church	Brown
Fairfield	The Church	
Fairford	Church	Brown
Fairford	Church & Mill	Brown
Farnham	Old Parish Church	Brown (late)
Felixstowe	The Church	
Felixstowe	(From the Cliffs)	Black
Felpham, Nr.Bognor	The Church	Brown, Black
Fenny Stratford	St.Martin's Church	Brown
Fermoy		Black, Colour
Filey	From the North	
Filey	The Parish Church	Black, Brown
Finchley		
Fishguard	The Harbour	Brown, Black
Flint	A Flint Mill	
Folkestone	The Boulogne Boat leaving the Harbour	
Folkestone	The Lees	Red, Colour
Folkestone	The Zig-zag path and Lees	
Folkestone	St.Mary's Church	Red
The Forth Bridge		Black, Colour (early & late)
Fountains Abbey		Black, Brown, Colour (late)
Fountains Abbey	The Abbey and Waterfall	Red
Frinton-on-Sea	The Beach and Promenade	
Freshwater Bay, I.o.W		
Furness	The Abbey & Ulverston	Colour, Black
Galashiels	Abbotsview Co-operative convalescent home and Eildon hills	Colour (late)
The Giant's Causeway	The Honeycomb	
Girvan	The Harbour	
Glastonbury	The Abbey	Black, Red, Brown
Glastonbury	The Abbot's Kitchen	
Glastonbury	St.Joseph's Chapel	Black, Red, Brown
Glastonbury	St.Joseph's Church	Red
Glastonbury	The Chapel of St.Mary, Glastonbury Abbey	Brown
Glasgow (1938 Empire Exhibition)	An Clachan Cottage	Colour (late)
Glasgow (1938 Empire Exhibition	North Cascade and Tower	Colour (late)
	Also: Buildings & Gardens	Colour (late)
Glenluce	The High Street	
Gloucester	The Cathedral	
Glyn Ceiriog	The Church	Brown
Gorleston	The Church	Brown
Gosport		Colour
Grange-over-Sands	The View from the Promenade	Black, Brown, Colour
Grange-over-Sands		Brown
Grange	From Cartmel Hill	Black, Colour
Grasmere	The Church	
Grasmere	The Lake	Red
Grasmere	St.Oswald's Church	Black
Gravesend	The entrance to Rosherville Tea Gardens	
Gravesend	Rosherville Gardens	
Great Marlow		Black
Great Missenden	The Abbey	Brown
Great Yarmouth	The Marina	
Great Yarmouth	St.Nicholas' Church	Brown
Great Yarmouth	The Waterways	Colour (late)
Great Yarmouth	The Town Hall	Black
Greenwich	The Gardens	
Greenwich	The Hospital	Colour
Gretna Green	Old Toll Bar	Colour
Groeslon	Brynrodyn Chapel	
Guernsey	Moulin Huet Bay	Black
Guernsey	Harbour of St.Peter Port	Black
Guildford	The High Street	Colour (late)
Guildford	The Old Town Clock & Hall, the High Street	Colour (late)
Guys Cliff	The Mill	Brown
Gwydr	The Castle	Brown, Black
Haddington	The Abbey	
Haddon Hall (Nr. Bakewell)		Black, Brown, Colour
Halesowen	The Church	Brown
Halesworth	The Church	

Chillingham Deer

York Gate, Broadstairs

Peveril Castle, Castleton

All Saints Church, Maidstone

Halifax	Methodist Church	Black
Halifax	Salem Chapel	Black
Halifax	Sion Chapel	Black
Halifax	Square Church, 1919	Brown
Hampton Court	From the S.E.	Black
Hampton Court	The Entrance	
Hampton Court	The West Front	Black, Brown
Hampton Court	The Lion Gates	
Harlech	The Castle	Brown
Harrogate	The Pump Room	Brown, Red, Black
Harrogate	The Royal Baths	Red
Haslemere	The High Street	
Hastings	Carlisle Parade, East Hastings	
Hastings	The Castle	Red, Colour (late)
Hatfield	The House	
Hawkeshead	Ann Tyson's Cottage, Wordsworth's Lodge	
Hebburn	New Town Primitive Methodist Church	Brown
Hebburn	The Jubilee of St. Andrew's Presbyterian Church 1923	Brown
Helensburgh		Black
Henley-in-Arden	The High Street	
Henley-on-Thames		Red
Hereford	The Cathedral	Red
Hexham	Abbey and Town Hall	Black
Highass Park		
Hindhead	The Gibbet Cross	Colour (late)
Hockerill		Brown
Holyhead	South Stack Lighthouse	Brown, Colour
Hoylake		Black
Hungerford	The Church	Colour
Huntingdon	St. Thomas' Church	Colour
Hull	Wilberforce House	Brown
Hursley	The Church	Black, Brown
Hythe	The Church	Brown, Colour
Hythe	The Canal	Black, Colour
Ilfracombe		Black
Ilfracombe	The Harbour	Black
Ilkley	Old White Wells	Brown, Black
Ilkley	The Bridge	Colour, Black, Red
Ilkley	Swastika Stone	Brown
Ingleton	Ingleton and Ingleboro Mountain	
Inverary	The Castle from the New Bridge	
Ipswich	Ancient House	Red
Ipswich	Wolsey's Gate, St. Peter's Church	Colour (late)
Ironbridge	Erected in 1779	
Isle of Man	Castle Rushen	Black
Isle of Man	Peel Castle	Black
Isle of Man	The Wheel, Laxey	Black
Isle of Wight	Map of the Island	Colour
John O'Groats	(without Cottage)	Black, Colour
John O'Groats	(with Cottage)	Colour

John Keble	His head printed above his signature N.B. Also found with 'Author of the Christian Year' on base	Brown, Black
Kelso	The Abbey, cloisters and War Memorial	
Kenilworth	The Castle	Black, Colour
Keswick	Friars Crag, Derwentwater	
Kettering	The Church	Black
Kilburn	The White Horse	Brown
Kildare	The Cathedral	Colour
Killarney	Muckross Abbey	Colour, Black
Killarney	The Old Weir Bridge	Colour
Killiecrankie	The Pass of Killiecrankie	Black
Kinghorn	The Sea Front	
Kingsbridge	The Market House	
Kingston-on-Thames	The Bridge	Red, Brown, Black
Kirkby Lonsdale	The Devil's Bridge	Colour (late)
Knaresborough		Colour (late)
Knaresborough	The Castle	Red, Black
Knaresborough	The Dropping Well	Brown, Red
Knaresborough	The River Viaduct and Church Tower	Colour (late)
Knaresborough	Goldsborough Hall	Black
Knighton		Black, Brown
Knighton	Broad Street	Black
Lacock	The Abbey	Brown
Laggan, Scotland	The Ship Canal	
Lancaster	The Castle	Black
Lancaster	The Gateway to the Castle	Black, Colour
Lands End	Two views	Colour, Brown
Lands End	The First and Last House (long version)	Colour
Larne	Black Cave Tunnel, near Larne	
Larne	Glencoe Village, near Larne	
Launceston	St. Mary Magdalene	
Lea Hurst	The Home of Florence Nightingale	Brown
Leamington	The Parish Church	Brown
Leamington Spa	The Church	Brown
Leamington Spa	The Mill, Guy's Cliffe	
Leamington Spa	The Royal Pump Rooms	Brown
Leamington Spa	The Town Hall	Brown
Ledbury	Old Market House	Brown
Leicester	The Hospital	
Lichfield	The Cathedral	Red, Colour (late)
Limpsfield	The Caxton Home	
Lincoln	The Castle	Black
Lincoln	The Cathedral	Brown, Colour
Lincoln	The Imp	Colour, Brown, Black
Littlehampton	The Pier	
Little Malvern	The Priory	Brown
Llanbedrog, Pwllheli	Glyn-y-Weddw	Brown
Llanberis	The Pass	Brown
Llanberis	View of Snowdon, the lakes and castle	Black, Brown
Llandaff	The Cathedral	Black, Red
Llandilo	Carreg Cennen Castle	Black
Llandilo	Dynevor Castle	Red

Old London Bridge, B.E.E.1924

Crystal Palace

Hythe Church

Sherborne Abbey

81

Llandilo	The Church	Red
Llandrindod	Avenue Pump House Hotel	Red, Black
Llandrindod	The Church	
Llandrindod	Shaky Bridge	Brown, Black
Llandrindod	The Rock House Hotel	Colour, Black
Llandudno		Black
Llanelly	Town Hall	Brown
Llanfairfechan		Black, Red
Llangollen	The Ladies of	Brown, Black, Red Colour
Llangollen	The Parish Church	Brown
Llangollen	Plas Newydd	Red, Black
Llanrwst	Church	Black
Llantrisant	The Castle	Brown
Llantrisant	Church	Brown
Llanwrtyd	The Bridge	Black, Brown
Llanwrtyd Wells		Black, Brown
London	Buckingham Palace	Colour (late)
London	The Crystal Palace (Both Towers)	Brown, Blue, Red
London	The Crystal Palace (R.H. Tower & fountains)	Red, Brown Black, Blue Green
London	The Great Wheel, Earls Court	
London	The Houses of Parliament	Colour (late)
London	Old London Bridge, the British Empire Exhibition, 1924	Black, Brown
London	Queen Victoria's Memorial and Buckingham Palace	Colour
London	North Cascade and Tower, British Empire Exhibition, 1924	Late colour
London	St. Paul's Cathedral	
London	Tower Bridge	Colour, Black
London	The Tower of London	Black
London	Trafalgar Square	Colour (late)
London	The Gardens, British Empire Exhibition, Wembley 1924	Black
London	H.M.Government Bldgs, British Empire Exhibition 1924	Black
London	The Indian Pavilion, the Wembley Exhibition 1924	Black
London	Victoria Bridge	
London	Wesleyan Methodist Church (Diamond Jubilee 1866-1926)	Brown
London	Westminster Abbey	Brown, Brown (late)
Long Eaton	War Memorial	Colour, Brown
Loughton	Free of the Forest	
Lowestoft	The Church	Colour
Lowestoft	The Harbour	Colour
Ludlow	The Castle	Black, Colour
Ludlow	The Castle and Church	Red, Black, Colour
Lulworth	The Cove	Brown (late)
Luton	St.Mary's Church	Brown
Lutterworth	The Church	Brown
Lydney	The Parish Church	Colour

Lyme Regis		Colour
Lyme Regis	The Cobb	
Lymington	High Street	Black
Lyndhurst	The Church	Brown
Lytham	Clifton Street	
Mablethorpe	Sailing Boat and Headland	
Madeley	The Old Court House	
Maidstone	All Saint's Church	Colour
Maidstone	The Bridge	Red
Maidstone	The Museum	Colour
Maidstone	The Palace	Colour, Colour (late)
Maidstone	The Town Hall	Colour
The Maldens and Coombe		
Malton	St.Michael's Church	Colour
Malvern	The Abbey Church (two versions)	Black
Malvern	Going Uphill	Black
Malvern	Coming Downhill	Black
Malvern	St. Ann's Well (two versions - with & without people)	Black
Manchester	The New Royal Infirmary	
Marazion	The Pavilion	Blue
Market Harborough	The Old Grammar Market School (Built in 1614)	Brown
Marlow	Church and Bridge	Brown
Marlow	Church, Bridge and trees	Black
Marlow	The Bridge	Red, Black
Matlock	High Tor	
Matlock	The Bridge	Black
Matlock	Derwent Parade	Colour
Matlock	Old Town	Colour
Matlock Bath	The Pavilion	
Matlock Bath	Promenade	Black
Melrose	The Abbey	
Menai Bridges		Brown
Meriden	The Cross, The Centre of England	
Mersea Island	Map of the Island	Colour
Middleton-in-Teesdale	A Fountain in the Park	
Middleton-in-Teesdale	High Force	
Midhurst	The Inner Front, Cowdray Ruins	
Midhurst	View from the South Road	
Milford	The Horse and the Water-mill	
Milford Haven	St.Ann's Lighthouse	Brown
Monmouth	Shire Hall and Rolls Memorial	Brown
Monmouth	Monnow Bridge	Brown
Monmouth	Monnow Gate	Brown
Morecambe	The Central Promonade	Colour (late)
Moreton	Old Moreton Hall	Black
Morgan Gold Mines, N.Wales	The Mill	Brown
Morgan Gold Mines, N. Wales	The Tramway	Brown
Morley	The Town Hall	
Moulsford-on-Thames	Boating on the Thames	

South African War Memorial, Wendover

Stonehenge

Marine Parade, West Cowes

Builth Bridge

Mount Sorrel, Lincs.		
Mumbles Head		Brown, Black
Mumbles Head	The Lighthouse	Brown
Nairn	Marine	Black
Nairn	Marine & Shaw's	Black
Nairn	Shaw's Hotel	Black
Nairn	High Street	Black
Nantwich	The Church	Black
Neath	Neath Abbey, South Wales	Brown
Netley	The Abbey	Black
New Abbey, Scot.	The Ruins	
New Forest	King and Queen Oaks	Brown
Newark	The Castle	Brown
Newark	The Cathedral	
Newbury	The Church and Memorial	
Newbury	Highclere Castle	
Newcastle-on-Tyne	High Level Bridge	Black
Newcastle-on-Tyne	St.Nicholas' Cathedral	Black
Newdigate	The Holiday Camp	
Newhaven	The Parish Church	
Newlyn	The Lighthouse and Harbour Entrance	
Newmarket	The Grandstand	
Newport, Salop	The High Street	
Newport, Pagnell		Black
Newton-Stewart	The Cree Bridge	
North Berwick	Tantallon Castle and Bass Rock	
North Walsham	The Market Cross and Bandstand	Brown, Blue
Northwich	The Swing Bridge, open	
Norwich	The Cathedral	Brown,Black,Colour(late)
Nottingham	The Castle	Black
Oadby	The Church	
Okehampton		Black, Colour
Okehampton	The Castle	Red, Black, Colour
Olney	The Church	Brown
Ongar	Fox	Colour
Ormskirk	The Parish Church	Brown
Osmotherley		Colour
Ossett	Town Hall	Brown
Oulton Broad	Three Views	
Overton	The Parish Church	Brown
Oxford	Christ Church	Red
Oxford	High Street	Red, Black
Oxford	Tom Tower	Red
Oxford	Magdalen College	Black, Red
Oxford	Market Cross	
Oxford	Adgates Dairy	Red
Oystermouth	The Castle	Black, Brown
Padstow	St. Merryn Village	Brown
Peel	The Castle	Black
Pembroke	The Castle	Brown
Penmaenmawr		Black
Penmaenmawr Village	Old Grammar School	Brown
Penmaenmawr	Dwygyfylchi Village	Brown, Black
Pershore	The Abbey	Brown
Peterborough	The Cathedral West Front	Brown
Peterborough	The Bishop's Palace and Cathedral	Red
Peterborough	The Cathedral N.W.	Black,Brown, Red

Pinchbeck	The Church	
Peveril	The Castle	Brown
Polperro	The Harbour	
Pontefract	All Saint's Church	Brown
Pont-y-Pridd	The Old Bridge	Brown
Poole	Free Library	Black, Brown
Poole	The New Inn	Black, Brown
Portland		Brown
Portobello	The Bathing Pool	Black, Colour (late)
Portchester	Castle Gateway	Brown
Portpatrick	The Harbour	
Portsmouth	The Town Hall	Black, Red
Portsmouth	H.M.S. Duke of Wellington	Black
Portsmouth	The Guildhall	Brown (late)
Portsmouth	H.M.S. Victory	Brown, Black
Portsmouth	H.M.S. Victory in Portsmouth Dock, as she appears today	Colour (late)
Portsmouth	Southsea Pier	Black
Potton	The Church	Brown
Poulton-le-Fylde		Brown
Press Heath	A View of the Camp	
Prestwick	Exterior of the Bathing Lake and the Car Park	
Princes Risborough	The Old Market House	Brown
Princes Risborough	Whiteleaf Cross	Brown
Purley	The Tram Terminus and Fountain	Brown
Pwllheli		Brown,
Pwllheli	Glyn-Y-Weddw, Llanbedrog	Brown
Raglan	The Castle	Black, Brown
Ramsgate	The Harbour	Black
Ramsgate	The Sands	
Reading	Broad Street	
Reading	New Grammar School	
Reading	St. Lawrence Church	
Redditch	Hewell Grange	
Redditch	St.Stephen's Church	
Reigate	The Church	Grey, Black
Reigate	The Castle Gateway	Grey, Black
Rhayader	Gareg ddu	Red, Green
Rhuddlan	The Castle	Black
Rhyl	Dyserth Falls	Green,Brown,Black
Rhyl	Dyserth Falls and Old Mill, Near Rhyl	Brown
Richmond, Yorks	The Castle and the Bridge	Black,Colour(late),Bro
Richmond, Yorks.	The Castle	Colour (late)
Ripon	The Cathedral from the South-West	Red,Black,Colour (late)
Risborough	The White Leaf Cross	Brown
Rob's Monument	See p.87	Black
Robin Hood's Bay		Colour
Rochester, Kent	The Castle	Red
Rochester, N'land		Colour (late)
Romsey	The Abbey Crucifix	Brown
Ross-on-Wye		Black
Ross	The Market House*	Colour, Brown
Ross	The Town Hall*	Black, Colour
	*N.B. Same building, but minor variations in transfer.	
Ruthin	Castle Entrance	Brown
Rye	The Pillory	Colour

Saffron Walden	Audley End Mansions	Black	Stamford	Burleigh House	Brown
Saffron Walden	The Church	Black	Stanhope		Black
St.Albans	The Clock Tower	Colour (late)	Stirling	The Old Bridge	
St.Andrews	The Castle		Stirling	The Castle	Black
St.Bees Head		Black	Stockton-on-Tees	Town Hall	
St.Helens	The Museum, Victoria Park	Brown	Stockton-on-Tees	Wynard Park	Brown
St.Ives			Stonehenge		Colour, Black
St.Ives, Hunts.	The Bridge	Brown	Stoney Middleton	The Church	
St.Michael's Mount, Marazion, Cornwall		Colour	Stranraer	The Garden of Friendship and the Pier	
St.Peters	Tower of Refuge	Black	Stratford-on-Avon	Ann Hathaway's Cottage	Brown, Colour (late)
Salisbury	The Cathedral	Brown	Stratford-on-Avon	The Church	Black, Colour
Saltburn		Colour	Stratford-on-Avon	Shakespeare's House	Brown, Colour (late)
Saltburn	Italian Gardens	Red	Sutton Coldfield	The Church	Brown
Saltburn	The Lower Promenade	Colour (late)	Swaffham	The Church	
Sandbanks	The Pavilion		Swanage	The Bay, looking South (This view may also be found entitled 'Swanage')	Black, Colour
Sandown	East		Swanage	The Church	Black
Sandown	West		Swanage	The Great Globe	Brown
Sandwich	St.Clement's Church	Black	Swanage	The Old Mill Pond	Colour (late)
Sandy	The Parish Church	Brown	Swanage	The Pier	
Scarborough	Castle Hill Barracks after Hun Bombardment	Brown	Swindon	Town Hall	Colour
Scarborough	The Spa	Black, Brown	Symonds Yat	The River and the Gorge	
Scarborough	Valley and Grand Hotel	Black, Brown	Symonds Yat	Station and River Wye	Brown
Scilly Isles	Tregarthen's Hotel	Colour	Tamworth	Ethelfleda Monument, Tamworth Castle	
Seaford	The Cliffs		Tattersall	The Castle	
Seaford	The Parish Church		Tebay	The Bridge and the Moors	
Seascale	The Crescent and South Cliff	Black, Brown	Teignmouth		Black
Seascale	Town	Brown	Teignmouth	From Torquay Road	Black
Seaton		Colour Black	Tenby	Castle Hill	
Seaton	The Church	Colour, Black	Tenby	The S.W. Gateway in the Town Walls	
Seaview, I.o.W.	The Pier		Tewkesbury	The Abbey, from the North	
Selby	The Abbey		Thaxted	St. Osyth Priory	
Selby	The Abbey Church from the South West	Brown, Black	Thaxted	The Church	Black
Settle	The Market Place	Colour (late)	Thirsk	The Parish Church	Brown
Shaftesbury	The Old Abbey Walls and Gold Hill	Brown, Colour (late)	Thornton	The Church	
Shanklin	The Chine	Black	Tintern	The Abbey	Brown, Black, Colour
Shanklin	The Church	Brown, Black	Tintern	The Abbey's interior, looking East	Brown, Black
Shanklin	The Old Boat House		Torquay	Walden Hill	
Shanklin	The Old Village	Colour, Black	Torquay	Vane Hill	Black
Shanklin	The Parade	Black, Brown	Totland Bay, I.o.W.	The Rustic Bridge	Black, Colour
Sherborne	The Abbey	Colour, Brown	Totnes	East Gate	Colour, Black
Shrewsbury	Butcher Row		Totnes	The Bridge (& steamer)	Black
Shrewsbury	The High Street		Tregaron	The Church	Brown
Shrewsbury	The Quarry		Troon	The Swimming Pool and Italian Rock Garden	
Shrewton	The Lock-up	Colour	Truro	The Cathedral from the North East	Colour
Sister Dora's Monument (See Walsall)			Tunbridge Wells	The Common	Black
Snowdon	The Summit of(& Train)	Brown	Tunbridge Wells	The Pantiles	Red,Brown,Colour
Southampton	The Bargate	Black, Colour	Tunbridge Wells	Toad Rock	Black (late), Black
Southbourne	The Cliffs		Tutbury	The Ruined Castle	
Southbourne	The Sands and Cliff		Tynemouth	The Aquarium and Sands	Colour
Southend	The Pier		Tynemouth	The Priory	Black
South Walsham	The Churches		Ullswater	The Head of Ullswater and Hotel	
Southwell	The Minster, N.W.	Brown, Black	Ulverston		Colour, Black
Southwold		Colour	Ulverston	Ulverston & Furness Abbey	Black
Southwold	The Church	Brown, Colour			
Southwold	The Gun	Brown			
Southwold	Gun Hill	Brown			
Southwold	North Cliff	Brown			
Stafford	The Castle	Brown			

Valle Crucis	The Abbey and Lake	Brown
Ventnor, I.o.W.		Black
Victoria Bridge	View of Victoria Bridge and Terrace	
Walberswick	The Church	Brown, Colour
Wallasey	The Abbey	
Wallingford	The Bridge	Red
Wallingford	The Market Square	
Wallingford	The Bridge and Church	Colour
Walmer	The Botanical Gardens	
Walmer	The Camp	
Walsall	Sister Dora's Monument	**Brown**
Wantage	King Alfred's Statue	
Wareham	St.Martin's Church	Colour
Wareham	St.Mary's Church and Priory	Colour
Warkworth	Castle and Hill	Colour (late)
Warminster	The Minster	
Warren House Inn		Colour
Warwick	The Castle	Brown, Black, Colour
Warwick	Kenilworth Hospital	Colour
Warwick	The West Gate and Leicester's Hospital	Colour
Warwick	The West Gate	
Waterford	Dungarvan Harbour	
Wellington	Christ Church	
Wellington	The College	
Wellington	The Cottage on the Wrekin	
Wellington	A Forest Glen	
Wells	The Cathedral	
Wells	The Cathedral from the South East	Black, Red, Colour (late)
Wells	The Cathedral from the West	Brown,Colour,Black
Wells	The West Front, Wells Cathedral	Red,Colour(late),Black
Wells	The Quarter Jacks of Wells Cathedral	Colour
Welsh Ladies Tea Party		Colour, Black
Welsh Lady		Colour
Wendover		
Wendover	View of the South African War Memorial	Light Brown
Wenlock	The Abbey	Red
Westbury	The White Horse	Brown
West Kirby	The Promenade	
Westport	A Present from Croagh Patrick	Colour
Weston-super-Mare		Black
Weston-super-Mare	From the Pier	Colour
Weston-super-Mare	Gardens and Pier	Black
Weymouth	(Beach & Bathing machines)	Colour
Whalley	St.Margaret's Range	
Wharton	The Hall	
Whitby	The Abbey	Colour
Whitby	The Harbour	Colour
Whitby	Captain Cook's Monument	Light brown
Whitchurch, Salop	St.Alkmund's Church	Brown
Whitchurch,Hants.	Laverstoke House	Brown
Whiting Bay	Whiting Bay and Holy Island	Black
Whitley Sands		Colour
Whitwick	The Monastery	
Wickham Market	The Parish Church	
King William IV's Coach	Was used by Queen Adelaide, an aunt of Queen Victoria, and later as the state coach of the Judges of Assize at Carlisle 75 years ago	Colour (late)
Wimbledon	The Windmill, Wimbledon Common	Brown
Wimborne		
Wimborne	The Grammar School	Black
Wimborne	The Minster	Black,Colour (late)
Winchester	The Cathedral from the North West	Black,Colour (late)
Winchester	The Cathedral	Colour (late)
Winchester	Cathedral from Avenue	Black
Winchester	The Church of St.Cross	Black,Brown
Winchester	The Westgate	Black,Brown
Winchester	The West Front of the Cathedral	
Windermere		Colour
Windsor	The Castle (Front and Cows)	Colour (late)
Windsor	Windsor Castle (from the River)	Colour (late), Colour Red,Black,Brown
Windsor	Windsor Castle from Eton	Brown,
Windsor	St. George's Chapel	
Witney, Oxon.	The Butter Cross	Brown
Woburn Sands	Henry VII's Lodge	
Woburn Sands	St.Michael's Church	Colour (late)
Wolverhampton	St.Peter's Church	Brown
Woodbridge	(From the River)	Black
Woodbridge	The Church	Colour
Woolacombe	Barricone Shell Beach	
Wooler		Black
Worcester	The Bridge and the Cathedral	
Worcester	The Cathedral	Brown, Colour
Worthing	Broadwater Church	Colour, Black
Worthing	Thomas A'Beckett's Cottage, West Tarring	Black, Brown
Worthing	West Parade	Colour, Black
Worsley	The Church	
Wycombe	The Abbey School	Brown
Wymondham	The Church	Brown
Wymondham	Market Cross	Black
Yarmouth, I.o.W.		Colour, Black
York	The Historic Pageant, July 1909	
York	The Minster, West Front	Brown,Red, Colour (late)

2. CANADA

Banff	The C.P.R. Hotel	
Banff	Rocky Mountain Goat	Black
Banff	Rocky Mountain Sheep	
Canada	The Highlanders of	
Coburg, Ontario	The Car Ferry	Brown
Coburg, Ontario	The Town Hall	
Cornwall, Ontario	The Old Fort	Brown
Fort William, Ontario	The C.P.R. Elevator "D"	Brown
Fort William, Ontario	Thunder Cape, Near Fort William	Brown
Goderich, Ontario	The Court House	
Goderich, Ontario	The Harbour	
Gravenhurst, Marysville	The Old Ford	
Medicine Hat, Alberta	The City Hall	
Medicine Hat, Alberta	Fifth Avenue Methodist Church	
Medicine Hat, Alberta	The Hull Block	
Medicine Hat, Alberta	Second Street	
Montreal	Christ Church Cathedral	
Montreal	The City Hall	
Montreal	The Lachine Rapids	
Montreal	Mount Royal Park	
Montreal	The Notre Dame Church	
Montreal	Place d'Armes	
Montreal	The Post Office	
Montreal	The Royal Victoria Hospital	
Montreal	St.James Cathedral	
Montreal	The Windsor Hotel	
Muskoka	(Indian in a Canoe)	Brown
Niagara, Canada	The Falls (Two versions)	Brown
Ottawa	The Chateau Laurier	Brown
Ottawa	The Houses of Parliament	
Port Arthur, Canada	The Collegiate Institute	
Port Arthur, Ontario	The Kakabeka Falls	
Port Arthur, Ontario	The Sleeping Giant	
Port Arthur	The S.S. Harmonic and the S.S. Moronia at Port Arthur Docks	
The Rockies*	Lake Louisa. *Originally issued as Lake Louise, Banff	
St.John, New Brunswick	The Admiral Beatty Hotel	
St.John New Brunswick	King Street	
St.John, New Brunswick	The Martello Tower	
St.John, New Brunswick	The Reversing Falls and Bridges	
Toronto, Ontario	The City Hall	
Toronto, Ontario	The King Edward Hotel	
Toronto	Parliament Buildings	
Vancouver, British Columbia	Hastings Street	Brown
Vancouver	The Hotel Vancouver	
Vancouver	The Lions	
Vancouver	Siwash Rock	
Winnipeg, Manitoba	The Legislative Building	

3. OTHER EMPIRE and FOREIGN

Adelaide(Aust.)	Railway Station and Torrens River	Colour
Barbados	Cassino, Barbados Aquatic Club	Coloured (on terracotta)
Berlin(Germany)	Statue of Friederich der Grosse (Frederick The Great)	
Cairns (Qld.)	Barron Falls, Cairns	Black
Cairns (Qld.)	Robs Monument	Black
Castel S.Angelo (Italy)		Colour
Christchurch(N.Z.)	Exhibition Buildings and Gardens (1906/7)	Black
Cupola (Italy)	Di S.Pietro E.	Colour
Enhuca	The Wharf	
Evangeline (U.S.A.)	The Old Church	
Falkland Islands	'The Great Britain', Stanley	Black
Holland	Scene of Dutch Children	
Holland	An Overland Dutch View	
Innisfail (Qld.)	Johnstone River	Black
Innisfail (Qld.)	Post Office	Black
Maroochydone(Qld.)	The River Front	
Maroochydone(Qld.)	Mrs. Stretton's Club Hotel	
Melbourne (Aust.)	The Exhibition Buildings	Colour
Melbourne (Aust.)	Ormond College	
Melbourne (Aust.)	Princes' Bridge and Flinders Street Station, from Alexandra Park	
Melbourne (Aust.)	The University	
Mildura (Aust.)	The Hass Hospital	
Mildura (Aust.)	The Chaffey Hospital	
New Plymouth(N.Z)	Pickekurd Park and Mt. Egmont	
Burleigh (U.S.A.)	Big Burleigh	
Burleigh (U.S.A.)	The Pacific Highway	
Burleigh (U.S.A.)	The Rocks at the foot of Big Burleigh	
Swabia (Germany)		
Sydney (Aust.)	The Harbour Bridge	Sepia, Brown, Green
Te Archa (N.Z.)	No.15 Spring	
Victor (S.Aust.)	The Causeway Victor Harbour	
Westphalia (Germany)		
Zuider Zee (Holl.)	Two Views	

J. Corps Regimental and Naval

The majority of the items contained in this section are scarce. Most of the specific Corps and Regiments did not have their arms emblazoned on Goss ware until the outbreak of the First World War. When hostilities ceased, interest, which was narrow enough already, waned with the general decline of the factory after the war.

Thus, with the scarcity of these decorations and the tremendous increase in interest in W.W.1 items, prices have risen rapidly. With the exception of the Army Service Corps (+ £10.00) and the two Camberley Colleges (+ £10.00, all the items listed below are + £25.00 – £50.00 depending on rarity, about which it is difficult even for the author to give an opinion.

All the Overseas Dominions, however, are + £30.00 – £60.00 Naval and Battleship crests are rare and + £40.00 – £60.00 should be added.

1st Life Guards
2nd Life Guards
2nd Dragoon Guards
4th Dragoon Guards (Royal Irish)
5th Dragoon Guards
6th Dragoon Guards
Coldstream Guards
Grenadier Guards
Irish Guards
Scots Guards
Welsh Guards
2nd Dragoons (Royal Scots Greys)
3rd Hussars (King's Own)
8th Hussars (King's Royal Irish)
10th Hussars
11th Hussars
XI Hussars (Prince Albert's Own)
14th Hussars
15th Hussars
18th Hussars
19th Hussars (Q.A.O.R.)
20th Hussars
12th Lancers
17th Lancers
Alexandra, Princess of Wales' Own Yorkshire Regiment
Argyll and Sutherland Highlanders
Army Ordnance Corps.
Army Service Corps.
Bedfordshire Regiment
Berkshire Regiment (Royal)
Black Watch
Border Regiment
Cambridgeshire Regiment
Cameron Highlanders (The Queen's Own)
Cameronians, The (Scottish Rifles)
Cheshire Regiment
Connaught Rangers
Devonshire Regiment
The Royal First Devon Yeomanry
Dorsetshire Regiment
Dorsetshire Yeomanry
Duke of Cornwall's Light Infantry
2nd Volunteer Battalion, Durham Light Infantry (all green)
The Durham Light Infantry
Essex Regiment
Glamorgan Yeomanry
Gloucestershire Regiment
Gloucester Hussars (Royal)
Gordon Highlanders
Hampshire Regiment
Hants. R.G.A.
Herefordshire Regiment
Hertfordshire Regiment
Highland Light Infantry

Honourable Artillery Company (Flaming Ball)
Huntingdonshire Cyclists' Corps.
Huntingdonshire Regiment
Inniskilling Fusiliers (Royal)
Irish Rifles (Royal)
Kent Regiment (East – 'The Buffs')
Kent Regiment (Royal West)
Kent V.A.D.
King Edward's Horse
King's Own Scottish Borderers
King's Own Yorkshire Light Infantry
King's Own Light Infantry
King's Royal Rifle Corps.
Lanarkshire Yeomanry
Lancashire Fusiliers
Lancashire Regiment (East)
Lancashire Regiment (South – The Prince of Wales' Volunteers)
Lancashire Regiment (Loyal North)
Lancashire (West) Howitzer Brigade, Royal Field Artillery
Lancaster Regiment (The King's Own Royal)
Leicestershire Regiment
Lincolnshire Regiment
Liverpool Regiment – 5th Battalion (The King's)
Liverpool Regiment – 6th Battalion (The King's)
Liverpool Regiment – 8th Battalion (The King's Irish)
Liverpool Regiment – 10th Battalion (The King's Scottish)
Liverpool Regiment, Comrades Battalion (The King's)
London Electrical Engineers
London Regiment – 4th Battalion (Royal Fusiliers)
London Regiment – 8th Battalion (Post Office Rifles)
London Regiment – 9th Battalion (Queen Victoria's Rifles)
London Regiment – 14th Battalion (London Scottish)
London Regiment – 15th Battalion (Civil Service Rifles)
London Regiment – 16th Battalion (Queen's Westminsters)
London Regiment – 18th Battalion (Irish Rifles)
London Regiment – 21st Battalion (1st Surrey Rifles)
London Regiment – 25th Battalion (Cyclists)
London Regiment – 27th Battalion (Inns of Court O.T.C.)
London Regiment – 28th Battalion (Artists' Rifles)
London Rifle Brigade

Manchester Regiment
Middlesex Regiment (Duke of Cambridge's Own)
Machine Gun Corps.
Motor Machine Gun Battery
Norfolk Regiment
Northamptonshire Regiment
Northumberland Fusiliers
Northumberland Regiment
Notts. and Derby Regiment (Sherwood Foresters)
Oxford and Bucks. Light Infantry
The Prince Consort's Own Regiment (Rifle Brigade)
Rifle Brigade
Royal Air Force (two varieties – one with laurels)
Royal Army Medical Corps.
Royal Artillery
Royal Artillery – Salisbury Plain
Royal Engineers (two varieties)
Royal Field Artillery
Royal Flying Corps. (two varieties)
Royal Fusiliers
Royal Fusiliers (10th Battalion)
Royal Garrison Artillery
Royal Horse Artillery
Royal Irish Regiment
Royal Scots (Lothian Regiment)
Royal Military College, Camberley
Royal Staff College, Camberley
School of Musketry, Hythe
Scots Fusiliers (Royal)
Scottish Horse
Seaforth Highlanders
Shropshire Light Infantry
Small Arms School, Hythe
Somerset Light Infantry
South Wales Borderers
Staffordshire Regiment (The Prince of Wales' North)
Staffordshire Regiment (South)
Suffolk Regiment
Surrey Regiment (East)
Surrey Regiment (East – Territorial Regiment)
Surrey Regiment (Royal West)
Sussex Regiment (Royal)
St. John's Ambulance Brigade (The Corps. Badge of)
Tank Corps
Warwickshire Regiment (Royal)
Welsh Fusiliers (Royal)
Welsh Regiment
Wiltshire Regiment
Women's Auxiliary Army Corps.
Worcester Regiment
York and Lancaster Regiment
Yorkshire Regiment
Yorkshire Regiment (West Riding)

Royal Field Artillery

Royal Artillery, Salisbury Plain

27th Batt. London Regt. Inns of Court O.T.C.

Royal Flying Corps

Royal Flying Corps (Wings)

Royal Engineers

Royal Engineers

Tank Corps

H.M.S. Hindustan

Royal Army Medical Corps

Army Service Corps

H.M.S. Superb

H.M.S. Colossus

2. OVERSEAS DOMINIONS 3. NAVAL and CRESTS of H.M. BATTLESHIPS

Yorkshire Regiment (West)
Yorkshire Regiment (East)

Australian Commonwealth
Military Forces
Canadian General Service Corps.
(Maple Leaf)
Canadian Engineers
Royal Canadians (The Leinster
Regiment)
Royal Highlanders of Canada
New Zealand General Service
Corps. 'Onward'
New Zealand. 1st (Canterbury)
Regiment
New Zealand. 3rd (Auckland)
Regiment
New Zealand. 4th (Otago)
Regiment
New Zealand. 9th (Hawkes Bay)
Regiment
New Zealand. 11th (Taranaki)
Regiment
New Zealand. 15th (North
Auckland) Regiment
New Zealand Engineers
South African Artillery
South African General Service
South African Royal Army
Medical Corps.

Royal Navy
Royal Naval Air Service
Royal Naval College, Dartmouth
Royal Naval College, Greenwich
Royal Naval Volunteers
Royal Marines

H.M.S. Achilles
H.M.S. Africa
H.M.S. Agamemnon
H.M.S. Antrim
H.M.S. Argyll
H.M.S. Audacious
H.M.S. Barham
H.M.S. Bellerophon
H.M.S. Britannia
H.M.S. Centurion
H.M.S. Collingwood
H.M.S. Colossus
H.M.S. Commonwealth
H.M.S. Conqueror
H.M.S. Cornwallis
H.M.S. Dominion
H.M.S. Dreadnought
H.M.S. Dublin
H.M.S. Fortune
H.M.S. Hercules
H.M.S. Hindustan
H.M.S. Indefatigable
H.M.S. Indomitable
H.M.S. Inflexible
H.M.S. Invincible
H.M.S. Iron Duke
H.M.S. King Edward VII
H.M.S. King George V
H.M.S. Lion
H.M.S. Liverpool
H.M.S. Lowestoft
H.M.S. Monarch
H.M.S. Neptune
H.M.S. Orion
H.M.S. Princess Royal
H.M.S. Queen Elizabeth
H.M.S. Queen Mary
H.M.S. Russell
H.M.S. St. Vincent
H.M.S. Superb
H.M.S. Surprise
H.M.S. Temeraire
H.M.S. Thunderer
H.M.S. Vanguard
H.M.S. Victorious
H.M.S. Warrior
H.M.S. Zealandia

See also Section M.2. Flags for
R.M.S. Ophir, H.1. for ship
transfers and N.7. for Non-
Naval ships.

Lincolnshire Regiment

16th County of London Queen's
Westminsters

The Suffolk Regiment

Oxfordshire & Buckinghamshire
Light Infantry

The Royal Sussex Regiment

2nd Vol. Batt. Durham Light
Infantry

6th Batt. King's Liverpool Regt.

Somerset Light Infantry

The Welsh Regiment

D.C.O. Middlesex Regt.

East Kent Regiment

London Rifle Brigade

Gordon Highlanders

Honourable Artillery Coy.

Royal Berkshire Regt.

Notts & Derby Sherwood
Foresters

91

K. Verses, Legends, Texts and Words

It is difficult to put a value on the multitude of items appearing under this heading. The Goss factory had a liking for the colourful prose of the time, indeed Adolphus Goss wrote several short verses himself.

A large range of teapot stands, milk jugs, beakers, loving cups, etc. are to be found with verses and the price shown against each item is only a guide to the extra value that may be afforded to a particular piece.

Words do not generally have any added value except Welsh, Gaelic or religious, which are + £15.00. The items which normally carry words, i.e. butter, cheese, hairpins, etc. will be found correctly priced in the Price Guide to Goss China by Nicholas Pine.

Usually found on the **Devizes Celtic Drinking Cup** is the following:-

The Market Cross, Devizes bears the following inscription:
"On Thursday, the 25th January, 1753, Ruth Pierce of Potterne, in this County, Agreed with three other women to buy a sack of wheat in the Market each paying her due proportion toward the same. One of these women, in collecting the several quotas of money, discovered a deficiency and demanded of Ruth Pierce the sum which was wanting to make good the amount. Ruth Pierce protested that she had paid her share, and said "She wished she might drop down dead if she had not." She rashly repeated this awful wish, when to the consternation and terror of the surrounding multitude, she instantly fell down and expired, having the money concealed in her hand."
+ £15.00

A Yorkshireman's Coat of Arms
A flea, a fly, a magpie, an' bacon flitch
Is t'Yorksherman's Coit of Arms.
An' t'reason they've choszen these things so rich
Is becoss they hev all speshal charms.
A Flea will bite whoivver it can.–
An' soa, my lads, will a Yorksherman!
A fly will sup with Dick, Tom, or Dan,–
An' soa, by Gow! will a Yorksherman!
A Magpie can talk for a terrible span.–
An' soa, an' all, can a Yorksherman!
A Flitch is no gooid whol its hung, ye'll agree,–
No more is a Yorksherman, don't ye see?

Plus Coat-of-Arms + £30.00

A Yorkshireman's Verse
Tak . Hod . An . Sup . Lad.
Here's tiv us, all on us.
Me an' all –
May we niver want nowt, noan on us,
Nor me nawther.
Copyright: Dennis & Holloway, Scarborough
+ £20.00

Verses, etc. (normally in Gothic script, with illuminated initial letter)
(a) **By William Shakespeare**
'Double Double, toyle and trouble,
Fyre burne and caldrone bubble.' (Macbeth)
(Found only on Witch's Cauldron'). See Price Guide, p.87

'Piping Pebworth,
Dancing Marston,
Haunted Hillbro,
Hungry Gratton,
Dodging Exhall,
Papist Wixford,
Beggarly Broom,
and Drunken Bidford.' + £15.00

'The quality of mercy is not strain'd:
It droppeth as the gentle raine from heaven
Upon the place beneath; it is twice blest;
It blesseth him that gives and him that takes:
'Tis mightiest in the mightiest: it becomes
The throned monarch better than his crowne.' (Merchant of Venice)
+ £10.00

'This above all –
To thy owne selfe be true;
And it must follow,
as the Night the Day,
Thou canst not then be false to any one.' (Hamlet)
(**Note:**– The foregoing is mis-quoted, and should read:–)
'This above all –
To thine own self be true;
And it must follow
as the Night the Day,
Thou canst not then be false to any man.' (Hamlet) + £10.00

(b) **By Adolphus Goss**
'Fil me with fragrant cyder I entreate
Made from fair Devon's appels pure and sweet
For cyder is the King of drinke I wote
No better boone to bless a thirsty throte
Nor rarer drafte can harte of man desire
Than this the boast of England bewtye-shyre.' + £10.00

'Goe not halfe way to meete a cuming sorowe
Butte thankful bee for blessings of to-day
And pray that thou mayest blessed bee to-morowe
So shalt thou goe with joy upon thy way.' + £10.00

'Of creamie clay the potter fashioned me,
That I with creamie milk might filled be,
With milk to make fayre ladyes face more fayre
And give strong men more strength to doo and dare.' + £15.00

'Seeke out the good in every man
And speake of all the best ye can
Then wil all men speake well of thee
And say how kind of harte ye bee.' + £10.00

The quality of mercy is not straind:
It droppeth as the gentle raine from heauen
Vpon the place beneath: it is twice ble st:
It blesseth him that giues and him that takes:
Tis mightiest in the mightiest: it becomes
The throned monarch better than his crowne.

Piping Pebworth.
Dancing Marston.
Haunted Hillbro.
Hungry Gratton.
Dodging Exhall. Papist Wixford.
Beggarly Broom. and Drunken Bidford.

This above all...
To thy owne selfe be true:
And it must follow,
as the Night the Day.
Thou canst not then be false to any one.

Seeke out the good
in euery man
And speake of all
the best ye can
Then wil all men speake well of thee
And say how kind of harte ye bee

Four Teapot Stands bearing verses.

(c) By Sir Walter Scott

'Grey towers of Durham . . . . . .
Yet well I love thy mixed and massive piles
Half church of God, half castle 'gainst the Scot
And long to roam those venerable aisles
With records stored of deeds long since forgot.' + £15.00

(d) By William MacCall

'Curved is the line of beauty;
Straight is the line of duty:
Follow the straight line
Thou shalt see
The curved line ever follow thee.' + £10.00
(Note:– The above verse is sometimes found with its first two lines
transposed, and lacking in author credit!)

(e) Robert Burns' Grace

'Some ha'e meat, and canna eat,
And some wad eat that want it;
But we ha'e meat, and we can eat,
And sae the Lord be thankit.' + £10.00

(f) By George Heath

(This verse is printed on the reverse of an urn carrying the
'Arms' of Rudyerd of Rudyard:–)
'Glorious Rudyard, gorgeous picture.
How I love to gaze on thee.
Ever fraught with sunny memories
Ever beautiful to me.
Whether storms sweep grandly o'er thee,
Light or gloom their charms impart.
Ever grand, sublime, majestic,
Ever beautiful thou art.' + £15.00

Illustrations, Accompanied by Verses or other descriptive matter:–
(a) **'The Farmers Arms'** (from the famous engraving by Richd. Abbey,
Liverpool Pottery, about A.D. 1794.)
'Let the Wealthy & Great
Roll in Splendor & State.
I envy them not I declare it.
I eat my own Lamb,
My own Chickens & Ham,
I shear my own Fleece & I wear it.
I have Lawns, I have Bowers,
I have Fruits, I have Flowers.
The Lark is my morning alarmer
So jolly Boys now
Here's God speed the Plough:
Long Life & success to the Farmer.' + £25.00

(b) The Old Horse Shoe

'May the good old shoe bring luck to you!
Good health and sweet content:
And may your path be ever blessed
With peace from Heaven sent.' Jno. Crowther

Below this verse would normally be a coat-of-arms, beneath which
would be printed The Legend. In cases where the arms are particularly
large, or some other decoration, e.g. four or seven flags, is used,
then the Legend is printed on the back of the model.

The Legend. The Horse Shoe has long been regarded as of great
potency against evil. All Europe believes, in a more or less degree,
that the hanging up of a Horse Shoe in the home is significant of Good
Luck. All the Kings of old up to the 13th Century carried out the
custom of having a Horse Shoe hung on the entrance of the Palace.
When the great St. Dunstan was asked to shoe the hoof of the Evil
One, he bound him up so fast, and so tortured him, that he had to
promise he would never enter a doorway over which a Horse Shoe
was hung. Lord Nelson, England's greatest Admiral, had a Horse
Shoe nailed to the mast of the 'Victory'. See Price Guide, p. 55

(c) **'Old Scarleit'** (depicting a grave-digger in a scarlet tunic and blue
stockings – and carrying the following wording beneath:– 'O[i]
(standing for obiit – he died) July 2nd 1594. R.S. aetatis 98.)

The following descriptive matter is normally included if there is
adequate space below or on the reverse of the item:–
'You see old Scarlet's picture stand on hie
But at your feete there doth his body lye.
His gravestone doth his age and death time show,
His office by theis tokens you may know.
Second to none for strength and sturdye limm
A scarebabe mighty voice with visage grim.
Hee had interd two Queenes within this place
And this townes house holders in his lives space
Twice over: But at length his own turn came:
What he for others did for him the same
Was done: No doubt his soule doth live for aye
In Heaven: Tho here his body clad in clay.' + £20.00
(From the wall of Peterborough Cathedral.)

(d) **'The Ripon Hornblower'** – depicted blowing his horn,
and surrounded with the words, 'Except ye Lord keep ye Cittie,
ye Wakeman waketh in vain.' + £5.00 small, £10.00 large.

(e) **'Robin Hood's Last Shot'.** (This decoration comes in two sizes –
the smaller version sometimes being placed on a model so small as
to preclude the inclusion of the appropriate verse:–)
'Give me my bent bow in my hand,
And a broad arrow I'll let flee,
And where this arrow is taken up,
There shall my grave digged be.
Lay me a green sod under my head,
And another at my feet,
And lay my bent bow at my side,
Which was my music sweet,
And make my grave of gravel and green,
As is most right and meet.' Two sizes: 35mm + £15.00, 75mm + £25.00

(f) **'The Trusty Servant'.** This decoration normally carries the
inscription 'A piece of antiquity painted on the wall adjoining to
the kitchen of Winchester College.' + £10.00. Larger pieces also
carry the following descriptive matter:–
'A Trusty Servant's Portrait would you see –
The Emblematic Figure well survey:–
The Porker's Snout – not Nice in diet shews
The Padlock Shut – no secrets He'll disclose.
Patient the Ass – his Master's wrath will bear:
Swiftness in Errand – the Staggs Feet declare:
Loaded his left hand – apt to labour Saith:
The Vest – his Neatness : Open hand his Faith
Girt with his sword – his Shield upon his Arm
Himself and Master he'll protect from harm.' + £15.00

Old Scarleits Verse

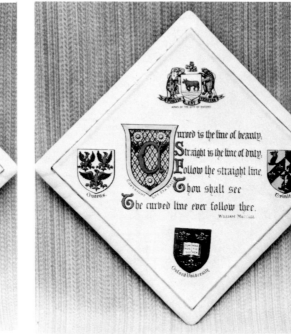

Sometimes the first two lines of this verse are in reverse order

Four Teapot Stands bearing verses.

2. WORDS

The Golden Dog, Quebec. A transfer print of which the background is 'brick-work' and centrally the picture of a dog gnawing a bone. The verse is in what appears to be early French-Canadian, and all punctuation is missing:—

'Je suis un chien qui ronce l'o
En le rongeant je prends mon repos
Un temps viendra qui n'est pas venu
Que je morderay qui m'aura mordu
Golden Dog – Quebec. 1786.' + £70.00

(h) **Rye** . (Normally found together with 'Seal of Rye' or some other local arms'–)
'Rye – The Romans named it "Ria" CDXLIX.
Saxons called it "Ye Anciente Towne of Rye".
Danes came with 250 Ships DCCCXCIII.
French burnt Rye and stole the
Church Bells MCCCLXXVIII.
Barons of Rye retaliated and brought
the bells back MCCCLXXIX.
Queen Elizabeth visited Rye and called it
"Rye Royal". MDLXXIII.
The Birthplace of the British Navy.
God Save Englonde and Ye Towne of Rye.'
(old Customal.) + £25.00

Sundry Victorian Texts (Usually in blue and turquoise Gothic script with illuminated capitals.)
The following are encountered, usually on 'lozenge-shaped' posy vases:—
'The Lord Is My Shepherd.'
'Let Not Your Heart Be Troubled.'
'Be Pitiful, Be Courteous.'
'Blessed are the Merciful.'
'Overcome Evil with Good.'
'Think and Thank.'
'None But The Brave Deserve The Fair.' + £10.00 each

'A Load of Mischief'
'Tis Thus I Travel on life's road
If bless'd or curs'd judge from my load.'
(From an old pottery engraving) with large transfer + £50.00

(A Seasonal Greeting)
'A Merry Xmas. A Happy New Year.'
(An ornamental diagonal cross with mistletoe in the four quarters and the lettering in Gothic Script superimposed.) + £35.00

Lincoln Jack (with correct inscription)
'1782 – City Ringers. This Jack was the gift of Alderman Bullen to the Company of Ringers.'
(Appears on a Lincoln Jack with blue and red bells). See Price Guide. page 60.

Beccles Ringers Jug
'When I am fill'd with Liquor strong,
Each Man Drink once & then ding dong.
Drink not to much to cloud your Knobs
Least you forget to make the Bobbs
a gift of John Pattman. Beccles (1827).' See Price Guide p.24.

Sundry Items of Wording:–

'The Green Immortal Shamrock from Erin's Isle' (Round ash/pin tray with Shamrock central) + £10.00
Wording from rim of Goss Agents' Dish :–
'Goss Original Heraldic Porcelain – Connoisseurs Collect It.' (See Price Guide, p. 181.)
Verse from **Hat of 'Churchill' Toby Jug** (Copyright 1927)
'Any odds – bar one
That's me who kissed
The Blarney Stone.' (See Price Guide, p. 175.)

Wording from plinth of **Cheshire Cat**:–
'He grins like a Cheshire Cat chewing gravel.' (See Price Guide, p. 106.)

Wording from **Lucerne Lion** :–
(on front) 'Die X Augusti II et III Septembris MDCCXCII'
(on back) 'Helvetiorum Fidei Ac Virtuti. Haec sunt nomina earum qui ne sacramenti fidem fallerent fortissime pugnantes ceciderunt soerti amicorum cura cladi superfuerunt.'
(See Price Guide, p. 106.)

Wording from base of **British Tank**:–
'England Expects that every Tank will do its Damn'dest.'(See Price Guide, p.29)

Wording from model of **Welsh Leek K.** Henry V. "The Welshmen did goot servace (At Crecy) in a garden where Leeks did grow." Shakespeare.

Wording from side of **Winchester Bushel:**
'Romsey. Jas. Mortimer Mayor 1722'.

Words
Butter
Cheese
Coren Ryfoeth Boddlondeb
Hairpins
Hair Tidy (two versions, one with rose, one with forget-me-not)
ihs (Red and Blue in Gothic lower case)
Hawod Roddloni Deowydd
Jam
Llanfair P.G. (The longest Welsh place-name which appears around the brim of a Welsh hat.)
Manners Makyth Man
Marmalade
Matches
Niwyr Dyn Ddolur Y Llall (One man knows not another mans pain.)
Pepper
Rhoddi Harddwch (Yield to beauty.)
Salt
Salt Vase & Pestle
Sugar
Tiodhlar Do Mhaise
Tobacco
Ychydig O Laeth (on Welsh Lady Cream Jug)

The Farmers Arms Verse

'Of Creamie Clay the Potter Fashioned Me'. A rare Adolphus Goss Verse

'Hair Pins' in Gothic Script.

Salisbury Gill decorated with 'RSM 1658' in red & blue lettering

Toilet Salt Mortar in red and blue lettering

With the reverse showing instructions by W.H. Goss in his own hand.

Witches Cauldron with a few lines from Macbeth.

The Wording on a Romsey Bushel

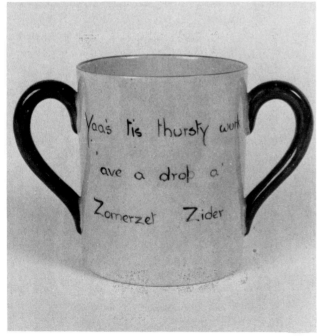

'Somerset' wording on a late two handled Mug

The Legend of The Old Horse Shoe

Most of the undermentioned decorations are very attractive early transfers and as such are valued at around + £50.00. They usually appear on 75mm mugs, often with blue handles and sometimes named. Exceptions to this are butterflies which are worth + £30.00 — £50.00 depending on the size of the piece, and seagulls which vary in price from + £10.00 — £30.00 depending on the number of birds showing. The final specific exception is the fox, 'Ongar', which is + £20.00

Bull
Butterflies — these can be divided into four categories.
(a) in gilt (with the addition of reddish-brown lines)
(b) in natural colours, with grasses
(c) single specimens in natural colour
(d) as (c) but on lustre-ware.
Camel
Cat and Bee (a decoration reputed to be by Adolphus Goss expressly for his children). 1, Contemplation. 2, Investigation. 3, Exasperation!
Cat, arched back, erect tail.
Cat, with kitten in mouth.
Chillingham Deer
Chillingham Wild Cattle
Cockerel
Dog (St. Bernard? — reclining)
Dog (Standing with blue bow)
Ewe and Lamb
Fox — 'Ongar'
Giraffe
Goat
Horse (Stallion)
Horse (Prancing)
Ibex
Manx Cat
Manx Rooster
Lamb
Lion, resting
Lion with prey
Ram
Rocky Mountain Goat
Rocky Mountain Sheep
Roe Deer
Rhinoceros
Seagulls
Sheep
Stork
Tiger
Vulture
White Mule, with saddle
Wild Bull
Zebra

Apples on a Cottage pottery mug

Butterfly Handled Vase. The handles are coloured blue.

Butterflies on a large Kendal Jug

Butterflies on a large Kendal Jug

2. FRUIT

Apples on a Branch
Blackberries†
Cherries†
Cherries on a Branch
Damsons†
Grapefruit†
Grapes, Red and white bunches of (early)
Lemons†
Oranges†
Plums†
Strawberries†
Unidentified Sprays of Coloured Fruit with green branches (late)
(Note: Decorations marked thus † can be found on Preserve Jars.
The lids of these can either have a white knob or a coloured one in
the shape of the fruit depicted on the jar. Value + £40.00. In add-
ition, the clover and bee decoration can also be found on Preserve
Jars. (+ £30.00).
The other decorations or any other fruit would add + £20.00
per piece to the value.

3. SEAWEEDS

The seaweeds are early and extremely rare designs. We have encountered seven varieties of seaweed — in varying colours: green,
pink and grey. Value + £40.00.

Cat & Bee 1. Contemplation

Early Moth Decoration

Camel

Prancing Horse

Cat & Bee 3. Exasperation
Phts-s-s-s !!!

Cat & Bee 2. Investigation

Wild Bull

Lion Resting

Seagulls

Grapefruit

Vulture ?

Zebra

Bees & Clover

Strawberries on a Preserve Pot

Manx Cat

These animal decorations are all
early and very colourful.

Manx Rooster

4. FLOWERS

(Note the majority but by no means all of the following must be considered late, i.e. post 1925.)

Anemones
Antirrhinums
Bay. Tree
Carnations
Celandines, with leaves in low relief (early)
Christmas Roses
Chrysanthemums
Clarkias
Clematis (three versions)
Clover (with bees)
Convolvulus (plain or blue)
Cornflower Sprays
Cosmos
Crocuses
Daffodils
Daisies
Delphiniums
Fern leaves in low relief (early)
Forget-me-Nots (late) (See also Section N.2 (a))
Harebells and Grass Sprays
Heather (large or small sprays) (See also Section N.2 (a))
Hollyhocks
Ilkley Heather
Killarney Fern, The
Life Plant — Bermuda
Lucky White Heather (late)
May Blossom. Possibly issued at the time of the engagement or marriage of Princess May of Teck to the future George V.
Manx Cushag (early)
Oleanders — Bermuda
Olive Tree ?
Pansies
Peonies
Poinsettias
Poppies (red, with green leaves — Jarrolds, Cromer, tea-set.)
Poppies (orange — hand-painted)
Primroses in Sprays
Primulas
Reeds and Flowers
Rose
Roses, Tudor (See also Section N.2 (a))
Roses on beige ground (late)
Saffron Walden Crocus (See also Section N.2 (a))
Shamrocks (See also Section N.2 (a))
Sunbeam Poppies
Sunflowers
Thistles (See also Section N.2 (a))
Thistle Sprays in red (late)
Tulips
Tulips (hand-painted)
Unidentifiable Spray of large mauve, blue and with green leaves
Violets
Wisteria

Once again, it is difficult to give accurate values in this section due to the range of items so decorated. Generally, however, + £20.00 per piece but rare decorations up to + £40.00, e.g. Saffron Crocuses, Bermuda Life Plant, Christmas Roses, etc.

See also Sections on Fruit and Seaweed which immediately precede this section.

Seaweeds – Seven varieties, all scarce. Usually found coloured red, green or grey.

The Killarney Fern

Bay Tree

Ilkley Heather

Poppies

Saffron Walden Crocus – Rare

May Blossom – often found with Princess May of Teck commemorative designs

Very colourful stylised Flowers (Late)

Primroses, Early

Anemones on a Butter Dish

M. Armour, Flags, Welsh, Shakesperian and Masonic
1. ARMOUR

Nine different designs were produced (all pre 1903) and were originally placed on specific models (in ochre yellow), viz:—

Ancient British Armour – Dartmouth Sack Bottle (large)
Assyrian Armour – Kendal Jug (large)
Danish Armour – Dartmouth Sack Bottle (large)
Etruscan Armour – Colchester Gigantic Wine Vase
Grecian Armour – Dartmouth Sack Bottle (large)
Norman Armour – Welsh Jack
Roman Armour – Abingdon Vase
Saxon Armour – Dartmouth Sack Bottle (large)
Scythian Armour – Lichfield Jug (large)

Obviously it is more desirable to have the appropriate armour on the 'correct' model (+ £50.00). Subsequently, items of armour, not necessarily including all items (such as helmets, daggers, etc.) were placed on other models. For example, the large Newbury Bottle is found carrying the breast-plates of two types of armour (+ £40.00). Again, small vases are found merely illustrating the smaller aspects of certain armours, and should therefore command considerably lower prices than the 'correct' models. (+ £25.00).

2. FLAGS and BURGEES

(**Note:** National Flags which have already been included in the 'Flags of the Allies' (Section H.3.) have been omitted here. Any apparent duplication of the above is because the specific flag indicated is found as a 'single' decoration.)

Australia
Canada
Chile (Blue flag with white central star)
Chile (Blue flag with white and red stripe)
Corinthian Yacht Club (The Clyde) – Burgee
Dartmouth Yacht Club
Egyptian Flag, sometimes with 'Alexandria' 'Cairo' or 'Egypt'
France
Greece
Guernsey, Flag of
Holland
India
Ireland
Italy
Japan, Flag of
Jersey, Ensign of
King Alfred, Banner of
Kirn Yacht Club
Lincoln, Banner of the Bishop
Mudhock Yacht Club – Burgee
Newfoundland
New Zealand
Oban Yacht Club
Portugal, Flag of
R.M.S. Ophir (Flag is wreath surmounted by crown)
Royal Clyde Yacht Club (Hunters Quay)
Royal Clyde Yacht Club – Burgee
Royal Dart Yacht Club – Burgee
Royal Dart Yacht Club – Ensign
Royal Highland Yacht Club – Burgee
Royal Highland Yacht Club – Ensign
Royal London Yacht Club – Burgee
Royal London Yacht Club – Ensign
Royal Southampton Yacht Club – Burgee
Royal Standard (of England)
Royal Victoria Yacht Club – Burgee
Royal Yacht Squadron – Burgee
Royal Yacht Squadron – Ensign
Rumania
St. Andrew, The Banner of
St. George, The Banner of
St. Patrick, The Banner of
Servia, Flag of
Start Bay Yacht Club – Burgee
Start Bay Yacht Club – Ensign
Union Flag ('The Union Jack')
United States of America, Flag of (showing 45 States)
Wales, Ensign of
Wales Flag of
West Kirby Yacht Club
White Ensign, The
Value + £5.00 – £10.00

Danish
The nine ancient armours

Roman

Saxon

Assyrian

Scythian

Etruscan

Grecian

Norman

Seven Welsh antiquities and
emblems

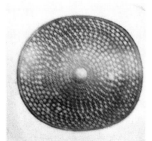

3. WELSH AND SHAKESPERIAN ANTIQUITIES and EMBLEMS

Black Welsh Hat with blue ribbons
Crossed Daggers (in yellow)
Crossed Leeks, surmounted by three converging black lines
Harp (in yellow)
Mistletoe on an Oak Bough, with golden sickle
Necklace (in yellow)
Prince of Wales Feathers in a Coronet
Red Dragon of Wales (The)
Town (or Station) Sign – 'O.Llanfairpwllgwyngyllgogerychwyrnd-robwllllysiliogogogoch'. (Rare + £50.00)
Shield (in yellow)
Welsh Goat (eating from tree)

Add £10.00 per item shown on the piece.

Note: There is also a Red Dragon of Wales, holding a knife, fork and spoon, and carrying the following inscription in a 'ribbon':

'Y Ddraig Goch A Ddyry Cychwyn', (The Red Dragon Gives the Lead) or 'Pa Le Mae Fy Nghiniaw?' (Where is my Dinner?) (See also B.N.7.). + £50.00

SHAKESPERIAN ANTIQUITIES

'Shakespeare's Arms'. + £40.00
Coloured bust of Shakespeare picture. + £40.00

4. MASONIC

(a) Functions

It was the custom in some Lodges to present a small Goss souvenir at their annual Ladies' Nights. We assume that most of these would have been retained by the recipients or their descendants, and therefore comparatively few have come onto the market. The following list is probably, therefore, far from complete. All these items must be regarded as scarce, by virtue of their limited editions, and rarer still due to the reluctance of present owners to part with their souvenirs. Alternatively, some may have found permanent homes in Lodge museums. For all Masonic items add £20.00 – £30.00:

1907. Concord Lodge No. 3239. June 15th 1907
1913. Concord Lodge No. 3239. Ladies Night, Feb. 15th 1913
1913. Abbey Lodge No. 432. Ladies Night, 1913
1914. Regents Park Lodge No. 2202. June 1914
1914. Royal Union Lodge No. 382. Ladies Night,4th Feb. 1914 (Uxbridge).
1915. Yenton Lodge No. 3464. Ladies Evening, December 3rd 1915
1920. Trisantona Lodge No. 3962. Ladies Night, Jan. 31st 1920
1921. Trisantona Lodge No. 3962. Ladies Night, Jan. 15th 1921
1921. Hatherton Lodge No. 2474. May 1921
1922. Trisantona Lodge No. 3962. Ladies Night, 7th Jan. 1922
1923. Trisantona Lodge No. 3962. Ladies Night, 6th Jan. 1923
1923. Trisantona Lodge No. 3962. Ladies Night, 29th Dec. 1923
1925. Trisantona Lodge No. 3962. Ladies Night, 17th Feb. 1925
1925. Trisantona Lodge No. 3962. Ladies Night, 27th Nov. 1925
1926. Trisantona Lodge No. 3962. Ladies Night,6th Nov. 1926 W.M. Wor. Bro. H. E. Morris
1926. Leopold Lodge No. 1760. Ladies Night, 5th February 1926
1926. Hartington Lodge No. 1085. Ladies Night, 13th October, 1926
1927. Hartington Lodge No. 1085. Ladies Night, 13th Dec. 1927
1927. Saint Werburgh Lodge No. 4147. Ladies Night. 16th Feb. 1927
In addition to the insignia or Banner of the Lodge and the date, usually a Ladies Night, the name of the Worshipful Master at the time or a particular Worshipful Brother will be found added.

(b) Emblems

The following signs and symbols are used in Lodge Ritual. They have not been exactly defined in Masonic terms but have been described here with a view to easy recognition by the layman:
(a) A five-pointed star, with various symbols inside the points; the word Fatal round the outside of an altar with an open book on it, with the initials C.E.S. on the side of the altar.
(b) Seven stars, a sun with face and rays, and a quarter-moon with face and beard.
(c) Compasses and a square, framing an eye in the sun's radiance.
(d) Builders' instruments incorporating a plumb-line, a level and a square.
(e) Implements as in (d) but in perspective.
(f) Eye in letter 'G'.
(g) Compasses, square, three columns, and chequered square paving.
(h) Five-pointed star, set between open compasses and a square.

(c) Masonic Arms, Seals & Crests

Abbey Lodge, Nuneaton. No. 432. Consecrated 1836.
Concord Lodge. No. 3239
The Grand Lodge of England (+ £10.00)
The Grand Lodge of Ireland (+ £10.00)
The Grand Lodge of Scotland (+ £10.00)
Hartington Lodge. No. 1085
Hatherton Lodge. No. 2474
Leopold Lodge. No. 1760
Regents Park Lodge. No. 2202
St.Werburgh Lodge, No. 4147
Trisantona Lodge. No. 3962
Warwickshire, The Seal of the Provincial Grand Lodge of
Yenton Lodge. No. 3464

Rare Masonic Symbols

Rare Masonic Design

Trisantona Lodge No. 3962 Ladies Night

The Stars

The Sun and The Moon

Abbey Lodge, Nuneaton

The Seal of the Provincial Grand Lodge of Warwickshire

The Royal Yacht Squadron Ensign.

Ensign of Jersey

Square, Compasses and Eye

Grand Lodge of England

Burgee Royal Clyde Yacht Club, Hunters Quay

The Royal Standard

N. Other Decorations

1. MARGARET GOSS

Margaret ('Peggy') Goss, daughter of William Huntley Goss, produced a number of coloured decorations, usually illustrations of nursery rhymes or animal caricatures for use on mugs and occasionally on plates. These were designed for children, and it is therefore surprising that even the small number we have seen still exist! All these decorations can be identified by a monogram comprising the letters 'M.G.' and bear the date 1922.

The Dancing Lesson. (Two dressed elephants dancing.)
Hey Diddle Diddle. (Cow jumping over the moon, the cat fiddling.)
Little Bo-Peep Has Lost Her Sheep. (Bo-Peep seated, crying with sheep scattered over the countryside.)
Little Miss Muffet. (Running from spider, with spilt bowl of whey.)
The Naughty Bear. (Crying bear being chastised by his elder.)
Oh For A Spoonfool. (Bear looking wistfully at honey pot.)
Poor Mince Pie. (Turkey, rabbit, goose, plum pudding and half-eaten mince-pie – all in black frieze round mug.)
Shopping. (Mother and daughter cats in human attire.)
Sweet Oranges. (Two pigs in conversation.)
Going For A Hop (Two kangaroos).
Farmyard Scene (with many Geese
Value of each piece so decorated £60.00

2. FORGET-ME-NOTS, THISTLES, SHAMROCKS, 'A PRESENT FROM ...' ETC.

(A) The decorations covered in this section are:–
    (i) Forget-me-nots
    (ii) Thistles
    (iii) Shamrocks (a) three-leaf
                  (b) four-leaf, with additional items
    (iv) The Tudor Rose
    (v) Manx Legs
    (vi) Heather
    (vii) The Saffron Crocus
    (viii) Leeks   (ix) Hunting Scenes

Note: For values of miniature items see Price Guide, p. 176

(i) Forget-me-nots
These are probably the most common decorations in this section, and two varieties may be found. The smaller, single-flower version as found on miniature and small items and a larger three-flower version used either liberally on bigger items or in conjunction with 'A Present From . . . . .' + £12.00. A third variation is found on the 'Initial' mugs, beakers, vases and jugs. The last-named items are sometimes referred to as 'Christening Ware'. and would certainly act appropriately as such, although possibly fragile in the hands of a young child. Over the years we have found specimens of all letters excepting Q, X, Y and Z. Possibly these also exist, but christian names beginning with these letters are far less common than the others. + £25.00

(ii) Thistles
These come in three varieties, two sizes of a one-flower version (the smaller one again being used on miniature ware), and a larger variation with two flowers and longer leaves. The larger single-flower version is also used in conjunction with, 'A Present From . . . . .' + £8.00, + £12.00 and + £18.00 respectively.

(iii) (a) Shamrocks – Three-leaf
There are three sizes of three-leaf shamrock, the smallest being used on miniature wares, the medium for general decoration, and the largest sizes normally in conjunction with 'A Present From . . . . . .' + £10.00

(b) Shamrocks – Four-leaf, with additional items
At least four sizes of this decoration are found, and comprise a four-leaf shamrock enclosed in an inverted horse-shoe, together with the words, 'Good Luck' beneath. Again, the three smallest versions are found on miniature items. + £10.00

(iv) The Rose
This may be described as a Tudor rose with leaves on each side, and normally found on items bearing also a thistle, a shamrock, and also occasionally, a crown. + £15.00

(v) Manx Legs
This decoration comes in two sizes, the smaller sometimes being used in conjunction with 'A Present From . . . . .' + £20.00

(vi) Heather
A spray of heather – in two sizes. + £10.00

(vii) The Saffron Crocus
This is the rarest decoration covered in this section, and has only been found on items bearing the wording, 'A Present from Saffron Walden'. + £50.00

(viii) Crossed Leeks
Only two examples seen. + £15.00

(ix) Hunting Scenes with horse and rider and three hounds, or with one hound. + £20.00

(B) The Uses of 'A Present From . . . . . .' and its variations.
Throughout almost the whole period of the firm's existence, it has been traditional to mark certain pieces 'A Present From . . . . . .' (followed by the name of a town or other location.) These fall into four categories – chronologically :

(i) In Gothic script – blue lettering. (Where the town name is lengthy, the words 'A Present' are sometimes omitted.)

An example of Terracotta Decoration

Terracotta Vase. Decorated with Greek key pattern.

An attractive **Country Cottage and Garden** shown here on a teaplate.

Forth Bridge. A Late colour transfer on a cake plate which also commemorates the Empire Exhibition, Scotland, 1938.

(ii) In Gothic script – blue lettering, but with the 'A', and the initial letter of the town in yellow on a red ground. (There may be variations of this colouring, as I have only had the opportunity of examining one specimen of this type.)

(iii) By far the commonest variety. this comprises the wording in 'sans-serif' capitals, 'A Present From' being above the appropriate emblem (i.e. (i), (ii), (iiia), (v), (vi) and (vii) as set out previously) and the place-name below. The words 'A Present From' are sometimes omitted, leaving merely the place-name.

Occasionally one is sufficiently fortunate to find an early tankard mug bearing not only the forget-me-nots, together with the full wording, but also bearing two coloured transfer-prints of animals. These are rare and should be treasured.

(iv) Latterly, copper-plate writing was used, usually in conjunction with hunting or coaching scenes, or with one of the later floral patterns (i.e. a rose).

The most common of the place-names found with these hunting scenes is Rye. Also found are Bishop Auckland, Brentwood and Southsea. '**A Souvenir From . . . . .**' is occasionally found as a variation of the above.

For any of the above wordings, add £5.00 – £10.00 depending on size.

Place names used with 'A Present From.......'.

See also Section G.4. for 'A Present from Wembley'.

These lists are far from complete – they may, however, be taken as an indication of the incidence of each type of decoration :–

(i) **Forget-me-nots**	(ii) **Thistles**
Andover	Braemar
Bowness	Brodick
Buxton	Burns' Monument
Chester	Crieff
Churchdown	Duke of Fife
Clacton-on-Sea	Edinburgh
Clare	Gatehouse of Fleet
Eastbourne	Gourock
Grange	Grantown-on-Spey
Hastings	Helensburgh
Hounslow	John O'Groats
Ilkley	North Berwick
Lichfield	Pitlochry
Matlock Bath	St. Andrews
New Barnet	Tignabruaich
Painswick	Whiting Bay 'Arran'
Pooley Bridge	
St. Columb Major	
St. Leonards	
Southend	
Teignmouth	
Torquay	
Tramore	
Wallace Monument	
West Kirby	
Westward Ho	
Windermere	

(iii) (a) **Shamrocks**
Belfast
Blarney Castle
Fermoy
Killarney
Monaghan
Sligo
Wexford
Also: The Green Immortal Shamrock from Erin's Isle.

A late, indeed modern transfer of a shamrock with 'A Present from Kenmare' has been seen. This may have been applied by the Agent as it is very doubtful that a piece so decorated ever left the factory.

(v) **Manx Legs**
Isle of Man
Port Erin
Port St. Mary

(vi) **Heather**
Bovey Tracey
Crystal Palace Opened 1854
Dolgelley
Glasgow
Hartington
Heacham
Heather Island (Lewis)
Killarney
From Land's End
Newton Stewart
Strathpeffer Spa
N.B. For Ilkley Heather see Section L.4.

(viii) **Crossed Leeks**
Mumbles
Newtown

(ix) **Hunting Scenes**
Bishop Auckland
Brentwood
Clovelly
Rye
Southsea

'A Present From . . . . . .'
(i) **Gothic Blue Script**
Bath
Bettws-y-Coed
Broadstairs
Buxton

(ii) **Gothic Blue Script with Illuminated Initial Letter**
Knaresborough
Much Wenlock
Ruthin

(iii) **'Sans Serif' Capitals**
See lists of Forget-me-nots, Thistles, Shamrocks, Manx Legs and Heather.

(iv) **Copperplate (late)**
Boscastle
Canvey Island
Cheddar
Clovelly
Llanfair Caerienion
Lulworth
Rye
Southsea
Tankerton
Woolacombe

Hunting Scene with 3 hounds 'A Present From Rye'.

Forget-me-nots. 'A Present from Clacton-on-Sea'

Forget-me-nots forming an initial letter.

Thistles. 'A Present from Gourock'

Hunting Scene with 1 hound

Rose. 'A Present from Rye'.

Shamrock. 'A Present from Blarney Castle'.

Heather. Strathpeffer Spa

Gothic wording, 'A Present from Ruthin'

Manx Legs. 'A Present from Isle of Man'.

Shamrock. 'Kilkenny'.

Shamrock. 'The Green Immortal Shamrock From Erin's Isle'.

Occasionally one may find a piece of Goss China decorated entirely in blue, including the rim. These decorations are normally of a patriotic nature, e.g. Arms of England, Cross of St. George, Tudor roses, thistles, etc. Almost invariably these models are marked 'Seconds' or 'Defective', presumably because the decoration has slightly blurred edges. This probably reflects some kind of First World War economy in the use of gilding and enamels – which does not seem to have been generally successful – hence the marking – and comparative scarcity. Value + £25.00 on smaller, + £35.00 on larger items.

'Awake, It Is Day'.

'A Merry Heart Goes All the Way' (with late floral decorations).

'Aberc Waen Nid Da Lle Gellir Gwell' (Abergwaun. It's not good enough when it can be done better).

Bees, in high relief on honey jar (Colour).

'Birds of a Feather Flock Together' (with late floral decorations).

Robert Burns (Coloured portrait).

Coaching & Hunting Scenes (frequently 'A Present from . . . . .') See page 108.

Cottage and garden full of flowers (Colour)

'Do or Die' . . . Royal Buff. Crocuses

'Do'ee 'ave a Cup of Tay' with crocuses (on tea pot).

'Don't Worry – It May Not Happen' (with late floral decorations)

'Droon Yer Sorrows'. From Ryde – with hand-painted design of tulips.

Forth Bridge (Coloured).

'Fresh from the Dairy' (with late floral decorations).

'Cymmerwch Gwpaned O De' (translation:- 'Have a Cup of Tea) – From Snowdon (on Welsh Lady Tea Pot).

'Ha, Ha, Ha, You and Me . . . . ' on Little Brown Jug.

'Iechyd Da I Chwi' ('Cheers' or 'bottoms up', a toast).

'I Love My Zider . . . . .' (verse on two-handled mug, with coloured apples).

'It's The Early Worm That Gets Caught' (with late floral decorations).

'Look Before You Sleep' (with late floral decoration).

'A Present from Caxton House, Limpsfield', normally accompanied by a black cat.

'Ride-a-Cock Horse to Banbury Cross' – with hand-painted scenes.

Shakespeare (Coloured portrait)

'Take a Cup o' Kindness' on late tea-pot.

Thistle (normal Goss mould) but with green glazed base, purple glazed trumpet, and red 1938 Empire Exhibition motif inside.

Three Cottages – Shakespeare's, Ann Hathaway's and Mary Arden's, all in colour with floral pattern between cottages.

Welsh Ladies' Tea Party (Coloured – on butter dish with wooden surround)

Welsh Ladies, (two) drinking tea – 'Greetings from Caerphilly'.

Weston-super-Mare Floral Clock Decoration (Colour).

Willow Pattern (normally on butter-dish with wooden surround)

Add + £5.00 – £30.00 for the above.

A Multi-coloured Lantern

Monmouth Mask. An example of the unglazed parian body.

Rye Cannon Ball decorated in black and brown

Denbigh Brick. White glazed with attractive decoration in relief.

Terra-cotta ware was decorated in at least five different ways:—

(i) Usually in black transfer and hand-painted conventional patterns, varying from floral to Grecian-style.

(ii) With classical figures in black transfer.

(iii) Bearing one or more of the following cartoons in black transfer:
'The Way The Money Goes'
'Wonderful Effects of Imagination'
'Working on Sunday'
'Caught At Last'   and possibly others.

(iv) Black-glazed with applied terra-cotta coloured classical figures. (This being extremely rare, and dating from the Goss and Peake period (1867)).

(v)(Probably much later) With the Arms of Barbados and an appropriate pictorial design.

For prices and illustrations of these pieces and decorations, see the Price Guide, p. 179.

Towards the end of the life of the factory, a range of colours was introduced on current models and domestic items to try to keep up with changing tastes. Add £10.00 for each.

The main colours issued were :—

Yellow (usually found with black trim)
Leaf Green
Dark Green
Black (matt)
Blue
Crimson
Red
Purple

In addition the following lustre colours may also be found:—

Lemon Yellow
Blue
Orange
Mother of Pearl
Rose Pink
Dark Purple
Pale Purple
White
Yellow

Bagware

Bagware comprises a range of domestic items in the form of a white 'bag' loosely tied at the mouth with a piece of cord, knotted to join the ends. The usual colour of the cord is blue although both green and red examples have been seen but are rare.

See the Price Guide 'Domestic & Ornamental Wares' but add £8.00 for green or red trim.

No Decoration

Some pieces were produced without arms or decorations at all — just white glazed. These items have no extra value.

Multi-Coloured Pieces

Many items were coloured by the factory in whole or in part and whilst they do not bear any particular arms or decorations are worthy of mention for completeness. Early parian figures were often trimmed with blue and gold. Occasionally red was used and sometimes the edges of dresses, etc. were just gilded. In addition, early scent bottles and vases were daintily decorated in blue, gold and red, and sometimes jewels were inserted, the process for this being one of W.H. Goss's earliest and most successful inventions. A preserve pot exists in the shape of a cottage, brightly coloured in red, black, yellow and white. A honey pot also appears found in the shape of a bee-hive, brightly coloured. Whilst these two pieces are very colourful they do not have particular decorations and are therefore indicative only of a range of products, usually later, which fall outside the scope of this book, but which will be found in the Price Guide, e.g., Flower Girls, Toby Jugs, Cottages, etc.

Gilding

Most products of the factory were gilded around the rim. On later pieces this 'gilding' or to be more accurate, colouring, was green, red, black or occasionally blue.

Sweet Oranges

Shopping

Little Brown Jug (Cottage Pottery). The lettering is dark brown with the first letters of words in red or blue.

Naughty Bear

Map of the **Isle of Wight.**

A Rose. Another example of Blue Goss

England. The Decoration and rim are coloured entirely in blue.

A Late **Floral Decoration,** on Cottage Pottery Mug.

A Late **Floral Decoration,** on Cottage Pottery Cup & Saucer.

Coloured **Powder Bowl,** with floral decoration.

Terracotta Jardiniere decorated with central band.

Glastonbury Salt Cellar in Mother-of-pearl lustre

Kirk Braddan Cross in brown washed parian

Bay Tree, The

Bear and Ragged Staff – 'R.L.'

Black Cat standing, within horse-shoe, with shamrocks, 'Good Luck', and verse as for 'Old Horse Shoe'.

Blue and Gold Dots (on miniature items). See page 176 in the Price Guide.

Cat and Fiddle Inn, Near Buxton. (The highest inn in England).

C.R. 1646 (on Salisbury Jack)

Dragon, green and yellow, holding knife, fork and spoon, with the following inscription in a ribbon beneath: Pa Le Mae Yr Ellmyn (translation – At what place are the Germans?) or Pa Le Mae Fy Nghiniaw (Where is my dinner?). + £50.00

Egyptian Frieze design, in black and white plus Greek key pattern, or coloured or red figures only. + £50.00

Excalibur

George and the Dragon

Lady Godiva, Coventry – picture of the statue; black transfer, with yellow sun.

Golden Dog, The – Quebec. (See also 'Legends' – Sect. K.l.)

John Greenway of Tiverton – The Merchant's Mark of

John Halle of Salisbury

John Halle – The Merchant's Mark of

Hairpins (on lid of rectangular box)

Henry, Duke of Warwick, King of the Isle of Wight. (Born 1424, died 1445) (See also Sect. B.l.)

Hereford Red Coat Man, The

Ilkley's Swastika Stone. Rare + £40.00

King Alfred's Banner

King Alfred's Jewel

King Arthur

King Arthur – from the Round Table at Winchester Castle

King Coel of Colchester ('Old King Cole')

Load of Mischief, A. (See also Verses – Section K.l.) Large colour transfer + £50.00

Man of War, Temp. Henry VII, A. (also known as 'Cinque Port Man of War') + £35.00

Map of the Isle of Wight. + £30.00

Map of Mersea Island. + £30.00

Match sticks – on lid of rectangular box and lid.

Monogram, possibly 'M and R' entwined (in turquoise blue) + £30.00

Jack of Newbury, – A.D.1550

Jack of Newbury, Arms of

Jack of Newbury – The Mark of (two versions)

Jack of Newbury – The Monogram of

Jack Smite the Clock

Old Scarleit (See also Legends – Sect. K.l.)

The Regalia of Scotland + £20.00

The Ripon Horn-Blower (See also Legends – Sect. K.l.)

Robin Hood's Last Shot (See also Verses, Sect. K.l.)

R.S.M. 1658 (on Salisbury Gill)

Rye, The Pillory. + £30.00. (See also p.84)

St. Cuthbert's Cross

St. Edward's Crown

St. George's Banner

Southwold Jack

'Star' decoration on large and small rosebowls.

The Trusty Servant (See also Verses, Section K.l.)

Warren House Inn – (The second highest inn in England).

Waterloo Memorial, 1815 (See also p. 68)

Welsh Lady standing by rocks (See (B) i.1.

William of Wykeham

Add + £10.00 – £20.00 for any of the above when **not** referred to another section with the exception of items priced individually.

Not since the early days of the factory when William Gallimore and Joseph Astley occasionally put their name or mark to certain pieces, has any reference to the identity of any particular modeller been apparent. With one exception, however, as impressed on the base of a hair tidy is the following: '12 March 1925 cast by J.T.B.'

8. SHIPS

All Late colour transfers + £30.00

R.M.S. Queen Mary

R.M.S. Queen Elizabeth

Early colour transfers + £45.00

R.M.S. Ophir

Jack of Newbury. A.D.1550

A Happy New Year. Merry Xmas.

Load of Mischief. A magnificent coloured pictorial.

Southwold Jack

117

Robin Hood's Last Shot. (See Section B.K.1 for verse)

The 'Pillory', Rye

Old Scarleit. (See Section B.K.1 for verse)

Hereford Red Coat Man

Ye Trusty Servant. Minstead

John Halle of Salisbury on Salisbury Kettle

Manners Makyth Man

Ilkley's Swastika Stone

King Alfred's Jewel

Stratford Sanctuary Knocker
– in relief.

Lincoln Imp outpressed on a
beaker.

M R Monogram (Blue)

Hairpins

Regalia of Scotland

Badge of The City of Exeter

Hythe Jurats' Seal

Merchants Mark of John Halle

Bear & Ragged Staff (R.L.
stands for Robert Leicester)

St. Cuthbert's Cross

Mark of Jack of Newbury

The Farmers Arms (See Section
B.K.1 for verse)

Crest of Sir Francis Drake

Man-of-War Temp. Hen.VII

The Price Guide to Goss China

Nicholas Pine

This is a completely revised edition of the original price guide by Nicholas Pine.

The new guide has much fresh information including numerous new pieces, many announced for the first time. A well illustrated domestic section clarifies this area of the factory's wares and improved layout and explanations make this chapter easier to understand and pieces easier to locate.

The dimensions of every piece are now given and the models section contains the correct matching arms for each piece - all separately priced. Prices have moved considerably since the publication of the earlier guide, a few down but most up - some as much as 200-500%. The very latest revised prices are given right through the book which is also a now virtually complete descriptive listing of every piece of Goss ever produced.

The guide is the standard work on Goss china and is used by the leading dealers and auctioneers.

The prices given form the base prices of pieces to which the values shown in this book for particular arms or decorations should be added.

The work is well illustrated and is superbly bound in hardcover with colour jacket. It is a pair with **The Price Guide to Crested China** and the sequel to **Goss China Arms Decorations and Their Values** by the same author.

Other titles on Heraldic China by

Milestone Publications

Please send for full catalogue

TAKE ME BACK TO DEAR OLD BLIGHTY
The First World War through the eyes of the Heraldic China Manufacturers *Robert Southall*
CRESTED CHINA
The History of Heraldic Souvenir Ware *Sandy Andrews*
PRICE GUIDE TO CRESTED CHINA *Nicholas Pine*
PRICE GUIDE TO GOSS CHINA *Nicholas Pine*
Arcadian Arms China Catalogue (reprinted)
The Goss Record 8th Edition 1914 (reprinted)
The Goss Record War Edition 1917 (reprinted)
Goss for Collectors - The Literature *John Magee*
A Handbook of Goss China *John Galpin*
Goss & Crested China illustrated monthly catalogues - available by Annual Subscription

ALSO IN STOCK
Let's Collect Goss China *Alf Hedges*
W.H.Goss and Goss Heraldic China *Norman Emery F.L.A.*
Heraldic China Mementoes of The First World War *P.D. Gordon Pugh*
The Price Guide to the Models of W.H.Goss *Roland Ward*

Milestone Publications
Goss & Crested China Ltd
62 Murray Road
Horndean Hants PO8 9JL
Telephone Horndean (0705) 597440